BEGINNING FRENCH WITH PRESCHOOLERS:

A MONTESSORI HANDBOOK

Rachel Adler-Golden
Debbie Gordon

Copyright c 1980 Montessori Workshop, Ithaca, N.Y.
Library of Congress Number: 80-83136
ISBN 0-915676-04-4

PREFACE

This manual describes a foreign language program recently instituted at the Ithaca Montessori Preschool in Ithaca, New York. Its goal was the introduction of French language and culture to the children in a manner designed especially for their age, needs, and capabilities. This project was geared to a group of nine 5 and 6-year-olds, the "extended day group," who spent a portion of their day apart from the younger preschoolers, working with advanced language, math, science, and other materials. The following pages will outline some of our activities with these children, and will make suggestions to those teachers interested in undertaking such a project.

It should be noted that our program developed within a Montessori, "open classroom" type setting. Although this influence may be evident in some of our activities, we believe that our approach could readily be adapted to fit other classroom settings—even the more traditional. We emphasize the fact that this manual is just a beginning; a point from which the individual teacher can depart, and, using his or her own creative impulses and imagination, can adapt and expand upon our suggestions to fit the particular needs of the children. We, too, will present our ideas for expanding our lessons to a broader and more involved program at the end of this manual. Because of our success and the interest our activities generated in the children, we feel that our experiences are well worth sharing. We hope that others attempting such a project will find similar results.

TABLE OF CONTENTS

PREFACE iii

I. INTRODUCTION 1
    Why Teach a Foreign Language? 3
    Organization of Lessons 5
    Materials 6
    Teaching Methods 7
    Suggested Sequence for Language Activities 10

II. LESSON PLANS 13
    Outlines of Activities 14
    Ideas for Expansion 65
    A. Toward an All-Encompassing Program 65
    B. New Units to Explore 66

III. APPENDICES 69
    A. Cultural Activities 71
    B. Cooking Projects 73
    C. Songs 77
    D. Books for Children 82
    E. Pen Pal Organizations 84
    F. Books for Reference 85

PART I: INTRODUCTION

WHY TEACH A FOREIGN LANGUAGE

"Why teach a foreign language to preschoolers?" many people ask. Some would indeed contest this idea, arguing that a second language is not directly relevant to the child's own experience, that the child will never use the new language, that the preschooler is too young to understand cultural differences, and that the experience is too confusing for a child who is trying to master his mother tongue. Despite these criticisms, we believe that there are many reasons for exposing a child to a second language at an early age. Here we will mention a few of them.

The first reason is in part a developmental one. Montessori explains that these early years, approximately ages 2 through 6, are a sensitive period for language development.[1] During this time, the child naturally and effortlessly absorbs language; in fact, this becomes one of his foremost preoccupations. Montessori also points out that once this period is passed, the child will never again be able to learn a language with such ease. She states: "Only children who in the age of infancy, that is, below seven years simultaneously learn several languages can perceive and reproduce all the characteristic modulations of accent and pronunciation of the different languages."[2] It seems logical, then, that a foreign language program should take advantage of this phenomenon, and introduce the second language during this sensitive period. Montessori, in *The Discovery of the Child*, describes how her young students easily spelled out foreign words after dictation.[3] Empirical evidence does, in fact, suggest that there are probably critical periods for learning a second language. It has been shown, for example, that those who learn the second language in their teens do not do so as "naturally" as the child, and usually retains some accent of their own language.[4] We were amazed at how well our children reproduced the French sounds, even though French and English phonetics differ significantly.

If the child is a natural imitator of the sounds around him at this age, why should his great abilities for learning be postponed until age 13 or 14, when he will no longer be as capable? The argument that the second language is too confusing did not appear to hold true in our program. Great care was taken so that learning French would not interfere with the learning of English. We did not deal extensively with the written word for example, so that the French pronunciations would not disturb our children's "sounding out" of English written words. We did not witness any confusion or deterioration in our children's English after exposure to our French lessons.

Secondly, learning a foreign language can have important cultural implications. On a world scale, increased communications and travel to remote parts of the earth have

---

[1] Maria Montessori, *The Discovery of the Child* (N.Y., 1967), p. 246.

[2] *Ibid.*, p. 246.

[3] *Ibid.*, p. 218.

[4] Ernest R. Hilgard, Richard C. Atkinson, and Rita L. Atkinson, "Langauge and Thought" in *Introduction to Psychology* (USA, 1975), p. 286.

caused our world, in a sense, to become smaller, while its problems, such as atomic war, pollution, and lack of sufficient energy, grow rapidly more universal. Therefore, we need to instill in its inhabitants, from the beginning, a sense of themselves as citizens of a world population. Mutual understanding and better communication among peoples of the earth is essential. Learning another's language is a vehicle by which this can be attained. We need only consider the stereotypical image of the American tourist, unable to communicate on foreign soil, yet annoyed that no one understands his words, to see how important language training is. Too often we Americans become unwelcome outsiders when we are abroad, because we can not properly express ourselves to native speakers.

On a smaller scale, learning about different cultures can help to eliminate prejudice, by educating children before inaccurate biases and stereotypes develop. In this way, children can come to understand and appreciate differences between peoples. A program like ours would be especially effective in schools where a second language is particularly predominant. In New York City, for example, where Spanish is widely used, children with English as the mother tongue may be started on a Spanish program very early. Here is an outstanding example of how better communication may be applied directly to the relationships between the children in the classroom. Subcultures within a school environment would not be so clearly delineated, if everyone could literally "speak the same language."

Although our children did not finish the year with a full understanding of what a different country is, they did have an appreciation for the fact that other children speak differently, go to a different kind of school, play different games, eat different foods, and so on. They seemed to have a natural curiosity about how others live, and this extended to even the finest details of everyday life. Once, for example, at our French tea party, we served the food on napkins due to a shortage of plates. One little girl sat silently for a few moments, and with a puzzled expression finally asked, "Do French people always eat from napkins?"

Thirdly, our French program seemed to give the children a better understanding of their own culture. Several bilingual children attended our school. One girl in the extended day class was raised with both Spanish and English spoken in the home. When we taught her the French word for something, she would often reflect for a moment and say, "I think it's the same thing in Spanish," or, "In Spanish that word is . . ." In the process of the lesson, she seemed to be discovering more about her own language as well. Similarly, learning about the activities of French children forced our own students to think more about their own activities, the kinds of food they like to eat, their family members, and so on.

Fourthly, our French lessons helped the children better comprehend the varied background of others in our classroom. Many of those in the extended day group were amazed to find out what a foreign language was—and also surprised to learn that some of their friends actually spoke another language! When we identified which children in our preschool class spoke two languages, some of the extended day children excitedly called them over and asked them to say a few words. The experience was also beneficial for these bilingual children who were not taking French lessons. These youngsters often felt uncomfortable about using their "other" language in the classroom. When we talked with them about different languages and countries, and when we asked them to help us with their own language, these children began to feel more at ease about using their mother tongue in front of us. Our interest pointed out that they had a skill to be proud of.

Why teach French to preschoolers? The final reason is simply that our children loved it. Our lessons were always optional, yet it was rare when we didn't have a full house. The children even began to ask for lessons during non-scheduled periods of the day. They seemed to enjoy acquiring and mastering a new skill. A certain confidence and satisfaction were evident as they improved with each repetition of the tasks presented. Our program instilled positive attitudes and "whet appetites" toward furthering language education. Many of the group, when describing the extended day program for a pamphlet we were preparing, mentioned our French lessons as one of their favorite activities. Mastering language was a game and not a chore for these children. Our materials were, above all, designed to be fun.

ORGANIZATION OF LESSONS

One of the most important factors in the success of our program was the fact that our lessons were optional. Our children were never expected to stop an activity that they were enjoying in order to attend, nor were they made to stay at our lessons if they felt tired and wanted to leave. It was this volunteer aspect of the lessons that assured that our French program did not become a tedious chore for the children. Work and concentration were required, but the work was perceived as entertaining because it was not forced upon the children.

After trying several different methods, we decided to divide our lessons in the following manner. Each child could attend class two times per week, once in a small group, and the second time with the large group. The small group was made up of three children and one teacher, and was basically a more intense session, dealing with old and new grammar, vocabulary and listening games, and other aspects of learning the language. We found that a small teacher-student ratio here was most effective, although the number of students in each group could conceivably be altered, depending upon the personalities, concentration, and abilities of the children. After working with the children and getting a feel for their personalities and capabilities, we grouped each child with the two others in the class that he seemed to work best with. Each small group progressed at its own rate. The large group lesson included nine children (all of the extended day group) and one or two teachers, and was geared to more cultural activities (stories, cooking projects, field trips, and parties) with some review of the material covered in the small group.

It is obvious that the more one is exposed to the second language, the quicker the progress will be. Adult students of a foreign language readily admit that fluency increases markedly when they travel to a different country and hear the new language all the time. Because of limitations on the availability of our two teachers during the entire preschool class's work time, it was only possible to schedule each child for two sessions per week and still maintain a favorable teacher-student ratio. It would of course be desirable, however, for each child to have the option of attending a lesson every day. Ideas for expanding our lessons to a full language "immersion" program will be discussed later.

The lessons themselves varied in duration. They could be short, from about 10 minutes, or long, up to a half an hour, depending upon the concentration and interest of the children. Lessons were always terminated when the children seemed tired. Children could also ask for lessons during our regular work time with the entire preschool class. They would often get together in a group of two or three and ask a teacher for help with one of our activities. Sometimes as many as 8 or 9 children would participate. Even our younger ones, ages three and four, played along with help from the older, extended-day children.

MATERIALS

Many of our lessons made use of concrete, manipulative materials, such as picture cards, objects, bingo cards, and so on which helped clarify the words taught. The materials were all hand made and simple to reproduce. This is an aid for both teacher and child, as less complicated materials are simpler to construct and easier for the children to deal with. It is important that the emphasis in each lesson be on the concepts to be learned and not on the intricacies of the materials. The material is only a vehicle by which to teach the concept. It is for this reason that versions of our activities were repeated throughout the course of the program. (We had, for example, three different versions of a bingo game, and two different versions of a grab bag game.) In this way, children were familiar with the use of the materials and needed only to concentrate on the new, French vocabulary.

Whether or not concrete materials were used in an exercise, we found that certain techniques almost always assured success. Physical, active involvement on the part of the children seemed to greatly enhance their interest. The commands game, where children held unusual positions of the body; the tea party, where children asked for and consumed food; the family pantomime game; the bingo game; the cooking projects; and many others all involved active participation on the part of the child. Strictly oral lessons with the teacher dictating at a blackboard (such as the kind of instruction an adult might have) were not found to be successful with our children.

We believe that materials should be accessible to the children whenever possible, so that they may practice with them during parts of the day when lessons are not available. In this way, the interested child may work on his own, with a tape recorder (see individual activity outlines), with another child, or with a teacher. When the child is working alone, a Montessori teacher may desire that self-correcting factors be introduced into the materials so that the child may check his own work. (The individual outlines will describe this process for those activities where it is applicable.) In cases where the child is working with another child or with a teacher, the others may provide feedback as to whether the child has answered correctly.

TEACHING METHODS

It is crucial to deal with subjects which are familiar to the children, and which relate closely to their own interests and experience. Our activities were divided into five units, starting with the child's own body, the family, and the foods they like to eat. Numbers (counting) and colors were also introduced, since the children were working with them elsewhere in the preschool and were fascinated by these subjects. Possible extensions of this familiarity idea might include, for example, vocabulary for activities that the chid likes to do (i.e. jumping, running, watching television, swimming, and so on). Whenever possible, the instructor should ask the children what words they would like to learn within a given unit of study. In putting together our body parts poster, for instance, we asked the children which body part they would like to begin with. The closer the activity corresponds to the child's own experience, the more interest he will have in participating.

It is also essential that the exercises given be short and clearly presented. We found that our grammar games typically lasted for ten minutes. We often presented several activities in a lesson, all dealing with similar grammar and vocabulary. Tasks within a given lesson should be varied, including some active and some quieter games (this, of course, should be determined, however, by the needs of the group on that particular day). Explanations of the rules of the game should be kept to a minimum. As Montessori aptly states: "The fewer the words, the more perfect will be the lesson."[5] It is for this reason that simple materials are preferred. The teacher should always keep in mind the goal of the lesson, and adhere strictly to obtaining that objective. "Getting off the track" is likely to be even more confusing to children than to adults.

Repetition is also critical in the learning of any foreign language—even for the adult. It is for this reason that we did not move on to a new exercise or new unit until the previous material had been mastered. The games, then, were repeated many times. In our system, a unit was never really finished, for a scheduled lesson might be devoted to one new activity and several of the older ones. The reader's initial reaction might be that repetition is probably boring for the young child; yet Maria Montessori's acute

---

[5]Montessori, *op. cit.*, p. 106.

observations and our own tell us just the opposite. In the sensitive period for any subject, the child will naturally repeat a chosen task again and again. It is through this repetition that the child obtains mastery over his environment.[6] Montessori comments: "If the object meets the inner needs of the child and is something that will satisfy them, it rouses the child to prolonged activity. He masters it and uses it over and over again."[7] Variations of the games are presented, however, in case the instructor wishes to expand upon the original.

Since repetition is the key to absorbing and understanding, some of the first games may be altered slightly and then repeated to work on different concepts. After the written word is introduced, for example, many of the old, oral games may be changed so that they involve some reading. The individual activity outlines will deal with this idea in greater depth.

As stated earlier, our lessons were presented orally for the majority of the program. Our children were already grappling with the intricacies of written English, and we felt that the French word, which uses the same alphabet but requires radically different pronunciations, would only confuse matters. Absorbing sounds, however, was very easy for our children, and their pronunciation was quite accurate.[8] The few written words given were introduced towards the end of the term, and we did not have the children sound them out; they were to be recognized only by "sight."

In presenting an oral lesson, we found it best to use gesticulation when clarifying the meaning of a French term. If this method was unsuccessful, we would give the children the English translation. We found it best, however, to minimize the use of English in order to emphasize the French words. When presenting the word "la tête," for instance, it is better to touch one's own head, repeat "la tête," touch the child's head, and perhaps repeat this again before one considers giving the English translation. The teacher might then say, "Show me 'la tête'," and finally, to see if the children can correctly remember and produce the word, point to her own head and ask "What's this?"

This is in keeping with Maria Montessori's idea of the three stage lesson which was adapted from the method of the French educator, Edouard Seguin.[9] The first stage is the association of the words to the concepts they represent. The second involves the child's recognition of the French terms, and the third involves the production or remembrance of the French word on the part of the child. Many of our activities make use of the three stages. In Body Parts Bingo, for example, the child has previously been given the names of the body parts (association). He must then mark the appropriate picture of the body part on his bingo card when he hears the corresponding French term. He can only do this if he understands what has been said to him (recog-

---

[6] Elizabeth G. Hainstock, *The Essential Montessori* (USA, 1978), p. 82.
[7] Montessori, *op. cit.*, p. 106.
[8] *Ibid.*
[9] *Ibid.*, pp. 156-158.

nition). After he has mastered these first two steps, the child himself may play the role of the teacher and become the bingo caller (production). This three step method is a concise and efficient way to proceed from listening or remembrance to actually speaking.

In keeping with our minimization of any detailed explanation, which we found to be confusing, we also avoided descriptions of grammatical rules. We did not explain the difference between the formal and informal subjects ("vous" and "tu"), nor did we go into masculine and feminine nouns, adjective endings or plural forms. Articles were always taught with the noun they modified. The children did not learn "tête," for example, but "la tête"; not "cou," but "le cou." No explanation of gender was attempted. It was emphasized, though, that the words "le" and "la" meant "the," so that the children would understand that the article and the noun were two separate words. Practice differentiating the article from the noun also occurred when the number unit was introduced. In several exercises, the child needed to modify a noun with a number, for example "cinq chemises." Here the child was corrected if he said "cinq la chemise."

In the majority of cases, though, the teacher would use the grammatical forms correctly with the children, but provide no formal correction when a mistake was made in any of these areas. When an error would occur, we would sometimes simply repeat the incorrect answer the child had given in the corrected form (doing nothing to suggest that the child had erred). In this way, the child could become accustomed to hearing the proper adjective endings, masculine and feminine articles, and so on, and would hopefully, after increased familiarity with the expressions, absorb the correction at some future date. Our program stressed the importance of repeatedly listening and eventually imitating what was heard. We felt that long-winded explanations of how to apply abstract grammatical rules would not be beneficial to the very young child.

The sequence of activities was essential in progressing from individual words to full sentences. We attempted to proceed one step at a time, starting with nouns of a certain vocabulary unit, and adding other parts of speech until full sentences could be produced. In general, we adhered to the following sequence: 1) First, nouns (and their articles) belonging to a given vocabulary unit were presented (ex. body parts). 2) Next, command verbs were introduced so that simple, but meaningful sentences could be formed (ex. "Touchez la tête"). These imperative forms were ideal, because they required no subject and could easily be added to the previously learned vocabulary. We started with verbs that sounded similar to their English counterparts[10] and gradually progressed to the other, less familiar verbs (ex. ouvrez, fermez, levez-vous, asseyez-vous, passez-moi, etc.). 3) After the command verbs, some adjectives (in this case colors) were taught to the children. These adjectives were first attached to the original nouns, and later, full sentences with the command verb, the noun, and the adjective were used (ex. "Touchez la chemis rouge"). 4) When the children had practiced this,

---

[10]We tried to use verbs that sounded similar to French ones whenever possible.

the first person subject plus a conjugated verb were used in limited cases (ex. "J'ai la chemise rouge"). Gradually the teacher began to use the second and third person subject more readily ("Jason a," "Elle a," "Tu as," "Vous avez," etc.), although the children were not yet required to produce these forms. Later a second adjective (numbers) with a different place in the sentence (the number adjective is placed before the noun, while the color adjective is placed after) was given. The children gradually construct longer and longer sentences. The children were soon able to express more complex thoughts.

Our activities, then, accentuated obtaining new vocabulary as well as ordering this vocabulary properly within the sentence. The very gradual progression of the single nouns to the full sentence facilitated a task which could have easily become overwhelming had it been presented carelessly. When new noun units were learned (ex. family, food), they could easily replace the old nouns and be fitted into the familiar sentences. (Ex. It was not difficult for the child to learn to say "J'ai deux soeurs" instead of "J'ai deux bras.") The children were beginning to absorb grammatical rules, although no such rules had ever formally been explained to them.

Naturally, we did not exactly follow the above steps, for we often introduced games, songs, stories, and other cultural activities, where unrelated vocabulary would come up. Expressions like "bonjour," "au revoir," "mes amis," "je m'appelle," "combien," "oui" and "non" were also dealt with in our program. It is important that children hear whole sentences and true conversation in natural contexts as well as practice the structured grammar lessons. As we mentioned earlier, the lesson plans must be flexible enough so that they cater to the interests and desires of the children, but rigid enough so that the exercises are leading toward certain clear objectives. In presenting a suggested sequence of activities, we underline the use of the word "suggested." The individual teacher may alter, add, or delete activities as he or she sees fit.

Furthermore, we do not specify where in the sequence to include the cultural activities. This is to be decided by the instructor. With these considerations in mind, we now turn to the outline and actual descriptions of the various exercises. The list entitled "Suggested Sequence" gives the order, purpose, and name of the activities, while the individual activity summaries describe the games in considerably more detail.

SUGGESTED SEQUENCE FOR LANGUAGE ACTIVITIES

A. *Introduction to France* (one lesson)
   1. Geography
   2. Culture
   3. What is a foreign language?
   4. Song: "Bonjour mes Amis"
            "Au revoir mes Amis"

B. *Unit I: Body Parts*
   1. *nouns*: Pierre Body Poster + Body Parts Record Book
   2. *nouns*: Bingo
   3. *nouns*: Blindfold Game
   4. *nouns*: Object box game
   5. *command verb + noun*: French Simon Says
   6. *command verb + noun*: Commands Grab Bag
   7. *review of nouns (plus additional vocabulary)*: Song: "Alouette"

C. *Unit II: Colors*
   1. *color adjectives*: Story: "The Red Balloon" plus color learning
   2. *adjectives (plus some command verbs)*: "Colors song" with balloons
   3. *adjectives*: I spy game
   4. *more adjectives*: Apple coloring and/or flag coloring
   5. *noun + adjective*: Balloon Card Game, Presentation A
   6. *noun (body parts) + adjective*: Color Bingo
   7. *command verb + noun + adjective*: Balloon Card Game, Presentation B
   8. *command verb + noun + adjective*: Magic Clothesline Game, Presentation A
   9. *1st person subject + verb + noun*: Balloon Card Game, Presentation C
   10. *1st person subject + verb + noun*: Magic Clothesline Game, Presentation B
   11. *3rd person subject + verb + noun + adjective*: "Oui ou Non" Game, Presentation A

D. *Unit III: Numbers*
   1. *numbers*: Number Bingo
   2. *numbers*: Numerical Grab Bag
   3. *numbers*: Rhythm Chants and Body Movement
   4. *numbers*: How Many? Presentation A, B
   5. *questions about numbers*: How Many? Presentation C
   6. *number + noun*: How many? Presentation D
   7. *1st person subject + verb + number + noun*:
      3rd person subject + verb + number + noun: Oui ou Non: Presentation B
   8. *3rd person subject + verb + number + noun*: How Many? Presentation E
   9. *1st person subject + verb + number + noun + color*: Monster Game
   10. *introduction of written word—number + noun + color*: number + noun + color book

Unit IV: Self and Family
   1. *Introduction*: Story: "A Week in Daniel's World" (see Appendix D)
   2. *expression "Je m'appelle" ("My name is")*: What's your name?
   3. *nouns (family members)*: Family coloring
   4. *nouns*: Family Pantomime Game

5. *1st person subject + verb + number + noun:*
   3rd person subject + verb + number + noun: Oui ou Non: Presentation C
6. *number + noun + color:*
   command verb + number + noun + color: Family + Adjective Card Game
   1st person subject + verb + number + noun + color:
7. *written word:* reading of familiar parts of story "Toute ma Famille" (see Appendix D)

Unit V: Food
1. *noun ("le pain"):* Trip to a bakery to watch the making of French Bread
2. *noun (foods):*
   command verb + noun: Food Card Game, Presentations A–D
   1st person subject + verb + noun:
   1st person subject + verb + number + noun:
3. *noun review + various verbs and expressions:* Baking French bread and making butter in preparation for activity number 4
4. *vocabulary from activities 1, 2, and 3 used in real life context:* French Tea Party

PART II: LESSON PLANS

TITLE: Introduction to France

PREPARATION: Assumes no previous knowledge

AIMS:

1) To introduce the concept of a "foreign country."
2) To introduce the concept of a "foreign language."
3) To explain that some people live very differently than we do.
4) To teach the children their first French words.

MATERIALS:

This may be left to the imagination of the teacher. Maps, such as the Montessori puzzle maps, or a globe may be shown to the children. Samples of French food may be brought in and some colorful photographs of France presented. Appendix D "Books for Children" suggests several picture books for this purpose.

A SAMPLE PRESENTATION:

1. The teacher discusses with the children cities, states, countries and continents, using the Montessori puzzle maps and/or globes. The children's native country and France are located, and the relationship between them is emphasized (i.e. distance between them, modes of transportation involved in going from one to another, etc.).

2. The teacher introduces the idea of different peoples having different customs and ways of life. Pictures are shown to help the children appreciate differences in clothing, housing, games, holidays, etc. Distinctively French foods may be served.

3. The concept of a foreign language is introduced. For example, it could be pointed out that if a French person were in the room, he or she would probably not understand what everyone was saying. The teacher could then speak some French and discuss the experience of not understanding, finally explaining to the children that they can learn to speak and understand this language.

4. The first French words are taught to the children: "Bonjour," "Au revoir," and eventually "Mes amis." ("Hello," "Good-bye," and "My friends.") The children practice repeating these words, and may also accompany the "hello's" and "good-byes" with waving motions.

5. The song "Bonjour Mes Amis" is taught to the children (see Appendix C).

VARIATIONS:

The teacher may complete this work in one or two lessons, depending upon the interests and capabilities of the children.

EXTENSIONS:

The teacher may go into more depth about family life, food, culture, or any of the other topics, or may bring in any number of teaching aids, depending upon the desires and abilities of the children.

POINTS OF INTEREST:

1) Learning about different countries and languages.
2) Learning the first words in French.
3) Singing the new song.

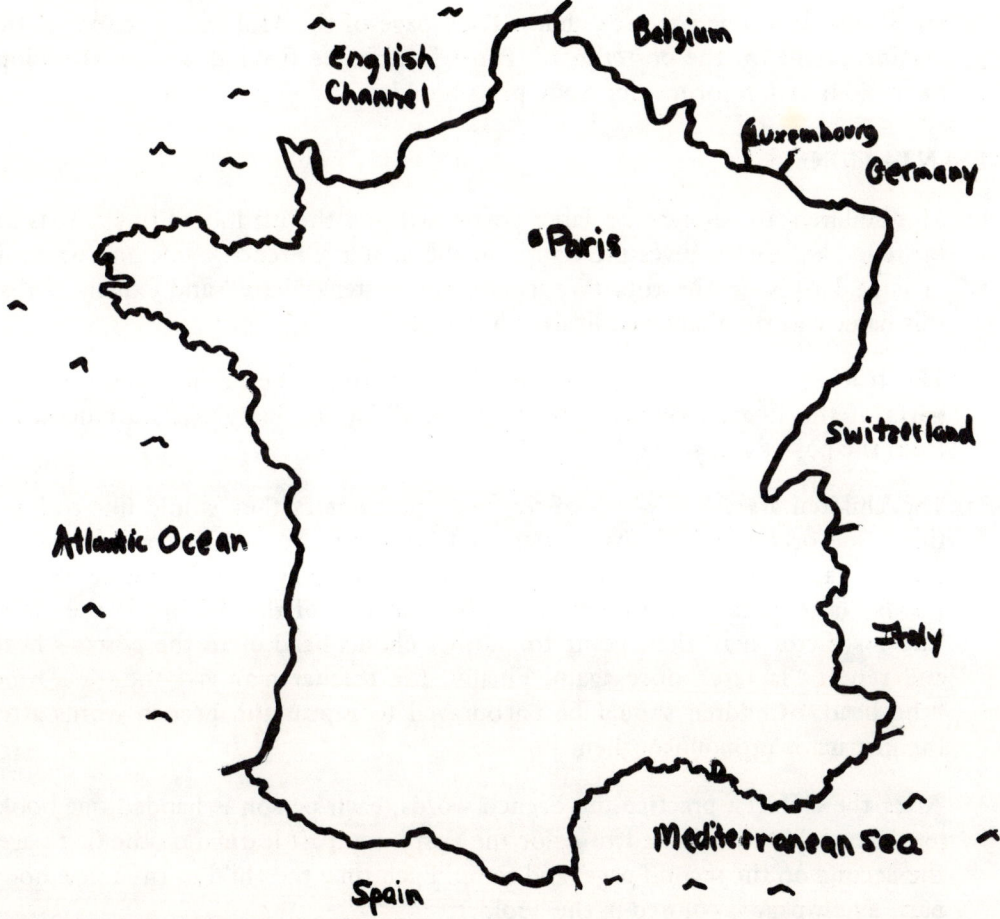

France

TITLE: "Pierre" Body Poster and Body Parts Record Book

PREPARATION: Assumes no previous knowledge

AIMS:

1) To introduce "body parts" vocabulary (nouns) to the children.
2) To review this vocabulary with the children.
3) To allow the children to keep a record of what they have learned.

MATERIALS:

1) A large flannelboard, on which the outline of a human figure is drawn.
2) Individual cardboard or felt body parts (ex. head, arms, feet, etc.) which fit perfectly into the outline on the poster. These should be attractive and brightly colored, and may be attached to the flannelboard with masking tape.
3) Small booklets (one for each child). Each page of the booklet is a replica of the outline found on the posterboard. Paper is available from Montessori Development Foundation for making body parts booklets.

PRESENTATION:

1) The children are shown the large poster with all the cardboard body parts attached. The teacher gives the figure on the poster a French name and writes it in large letters on the top. (We named our poster "Pierre" and explained that this name was the French equivalent of "Peter.")

2) The teacher explains that everyone will be learning the French names for the parts of the figure's (Pierre's) body. Then all of the body parts are detached from the poster and set aside.

3) The children are asked which of the body part names they would like to learn first. One or two of the parts suggested are reattached to the poster and the French names are given to the children. The teacher may, for example, say the words "la tête" and then point to the head of one of the children in the room. The instructor may then point to another child's head or to the poster's head and repeat "la tête" once again. Finally, the teacher may give the translation "the head." Children should be encouraged to repeat the French words after the instructor pronounces them.

4) After the children practice the French words, each person is handed one booklet. The child is instructed to color the first body part learned on the first page, the second on the second page, and so on. Each time the child learns a new body part, a new page is colored in the booklet.

5) During the next few lessons, old body parts are reviewed and several new ones are presented. This activity may be given in conjunction with other activities or may be put aside for a while and then returned to when the children are ready for some new vocabulary.

6) When the children have finished learning all the body parts, they may complete the last page of their book. This final page is a picture of the figure with all the body parts colored in.

VARIATIONS:

After several body parts are learned, the teacher has the children study the poster and close their eyes. One of the body parts is then removed from the picture and hidden from the children. The class must then call out the French name for the part that is missing.

EXTENSIONS:

1) Names of clothing may be used in addition to names of body parts.
2) Later on, when written words are introduced, the children may write (with the teacher's aid) the name of the body part under each picture in the booklet.
3) Individual sheets may also be prepared, each one with a different French name underneath a picture outline. The children may choose any one of these sheets, read the word which is printed, and color the appropriate body part.

POINTS OF INTEREST:

1) Seeing the amusing and colorful picture of "Pierre."
2) Watching Pierre gradually get rebuilt.
3) Filling up the "private" booklets, which correspond to the poster.

DESIGN CUES:

Learning is aided by both the visual aspect of the poster and the booklets, and by the activity of coloring the various body parts. The booklets offer the children a record of what they have learned, and provide a good aid for private practice with the new vocabulary.

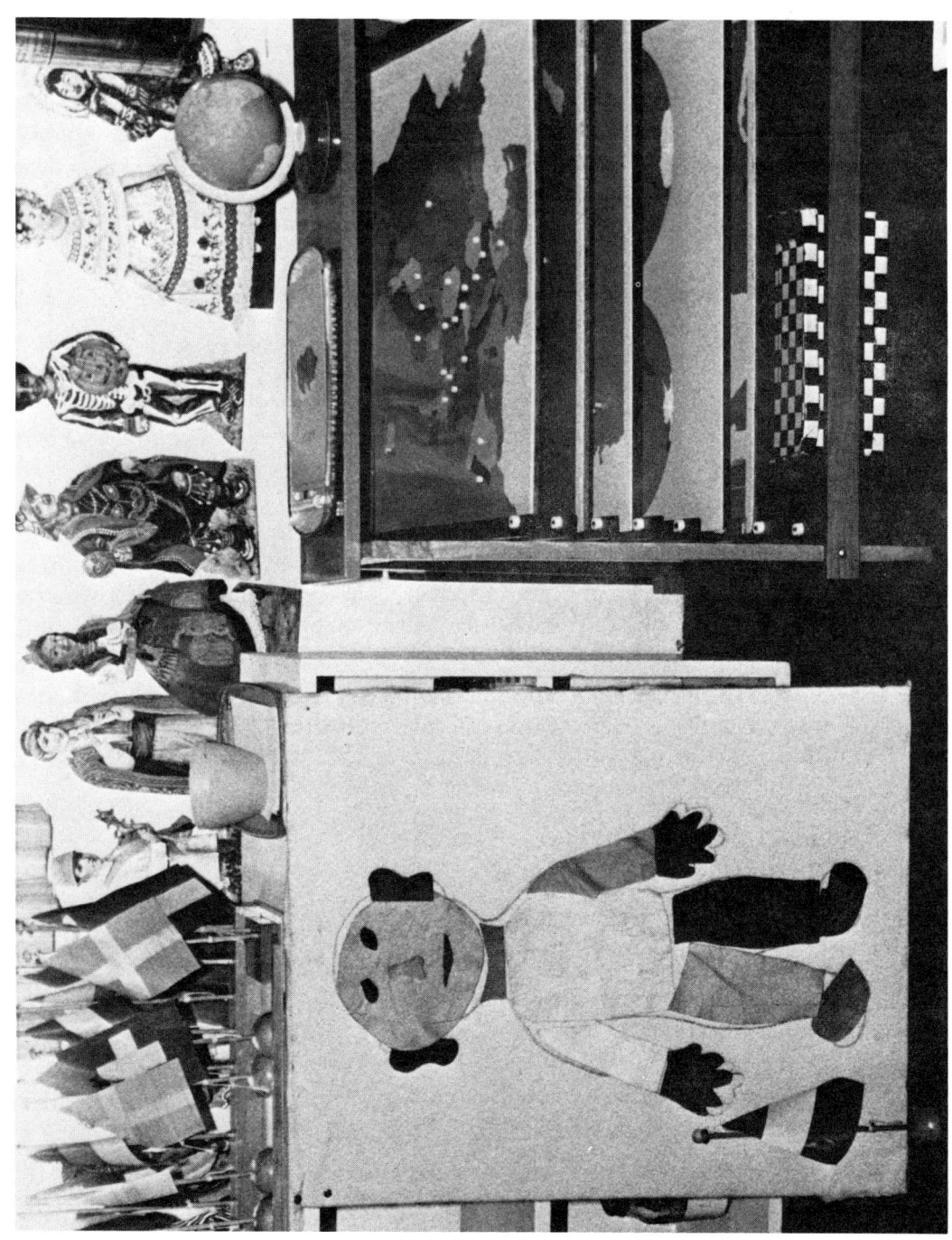

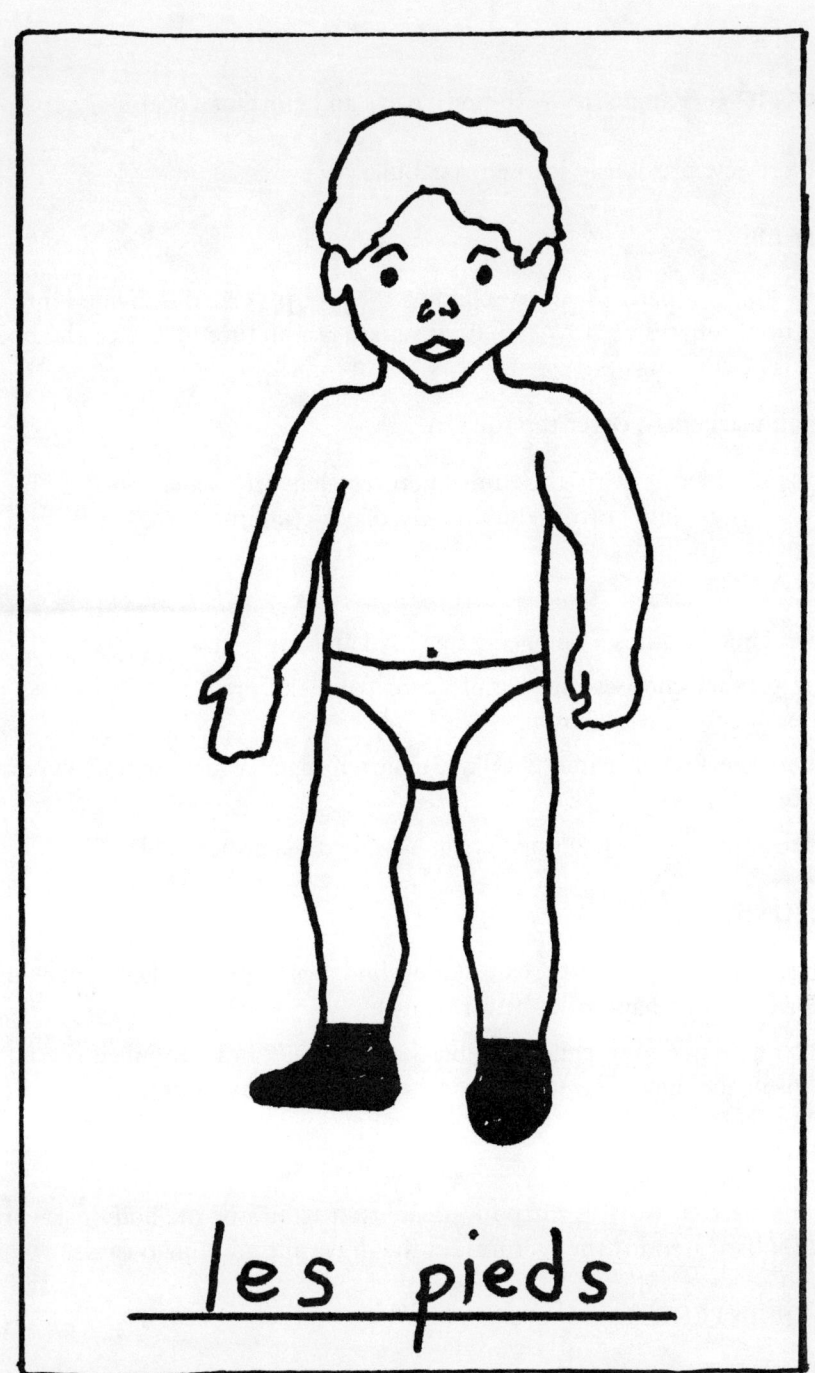

TITLE: Bingo

PREPARATION: Familiarity with body parts and clothing vocabulary

AIMS: To review previously learned vocabulary

MATERIALS:

1) One "bingo" card for every child in the group. A card is divided into three rows of three squares each. Within each square is a picture of one of the body parts or items of clothing.
2) Small markers to cover the squares.
3) Individual cards with the same pictures that are drawn on the "bingo" cards. These "draw pile" cards contain only one picture per card.

PRESENTATION:

1) Each child chooses a "bingo" game card and some markers.
2) The teacher chooses one picture card from the draw pile and states the French name for what was chosen.
3) When the French name is called, children place a marker on the corresponding picture.
4) The game is over when one person has filled his or her card.

VARIATIONS:

1) The game may be over when one child has three markers lined up in a row (horizontally, diagonally, or vertically).
2) After practice, one child may be the "leader," and announce the names of the cards in the draw pile, while the other children play as before.

EXTENSIONS:

After the written word is introduced, written names of the body parts and clothing may be substituted for the pictures on the draw pile and bingo cards.

POINTS OF INTEREST:

1) The attractiveness of the pictures.
2) The placement of the markers on the pictures.
3) The social aspects of playing a game with other children.

DESIGN CUES:

1) Repetition of the pictures.
2) The use of picture cards in the draw pile. This enables the child to assume the role of the teacher in variation 2.

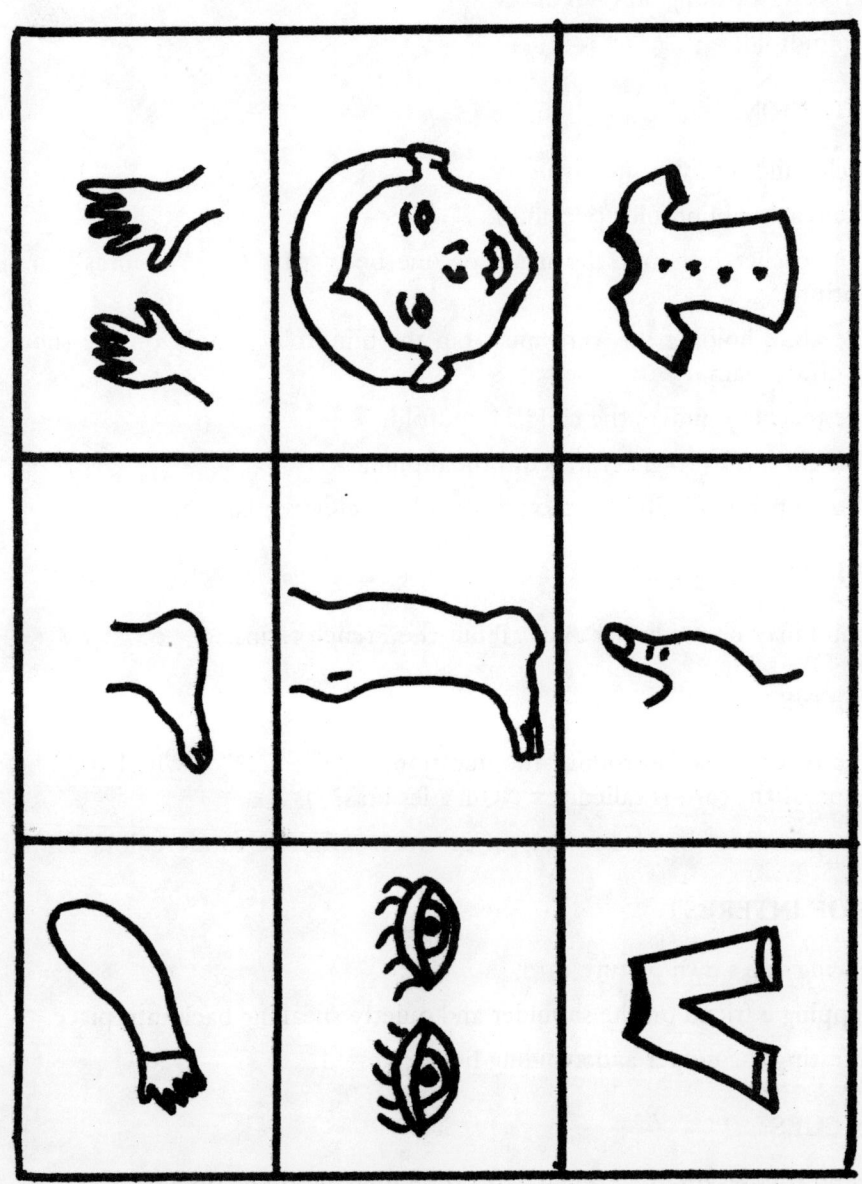

TITLE: Blindfold Game

PREPARATION: Familiarity with body parts and clothing vocabulary

AIMS: Review of body parts and clothing vocabulary

MATERIALS:

1) A set of cards (each approximately 4" x 6") with pictures of individual body parts and clothing on each one.
2) A blindfold.

PRESENTATION:

1) Each child receives one card.
2) The teacher blindfolds one child.
3) The teacher calls out the name of one body part (ex. "les bras") or item of clothing.
4) The child holding this card must tap the blindfolded child on the shoulder and sit down again.
5) The teacher removes the child's blindfold.
6) This child tries to guess who did the tapping.
7) The tapper is blindfolded next, until all the children have had a turn.

VARIATIONS:

One child may be the leader and call out the French terms.

EXTENSIONS:

1) The teacher may introduce the question, "Qui a . . .?" ("Who has?") before the name of the card is called (ex. "Qui a les bras?").
2) This game may be used for any of the other units (ex. foods, colors, family, etc.).

POINTS OF INTEREST:

1) Having one's own picture card.
2) Tapping a friend on the shoulder and quietly sneaking back into place.
3) Guessing the tapper and avoiding being guessed.

DESIGN CUES:

The child focuses on one French word for a long period of time.

TITLE: Object Box Game

PREPARATION: Familiarity with body parts vocabulary

AIMS: Review of body parts vocabulary

MATERIALS:

1) Objects (or pictures of objects) representing the body parts that have been learned.
2) A large cardboard box in which the objects are placed.
3) A blindfold.

PRESENTATION:

1) Child number 1 is blindfolded.
2) Child number 2 chooses one object from the box. This child describes what the object does. (Ex. for "le pied," the child might say "it walks," or "it jumps.")
3) Child number 1 must guess in French the name of the object.
4) The blindfold is removed and the object is presented to the child so that he may see if he has guessed correctly.
5) All the children take turns.

VARIATIONS:

1) One object is removed from the box while the children hide their eyes. The children must guess in French which object is missing.
2) A blindfolded child may reach into the box, feel an object and announce its French name to the class.

EXTENSIONS:

After the written word is introduced, cards with the written French terms may be substituted for the objects.

POINTS OF INTEREST:

1) The attractiveness of the objects.
2) The freedom to choose one's favorite object.
3) The feeling of the objects and the attempts to guess what they are.

DESIGN CUES:

The child must focus on the name of one object for a considerable length of time.

TITLE: French Simon Says

PREPARATION: Familiarity with body parts and clothing vocabulary
Familiarity with Simon Says game in English

AIMS:

1) To use previously learned vocabulary in a meaningful context.
2) To introduce full sentences using command verbs.

MATERIALS: None required

PRESENTATION:

1) The teacher explains the words "Touchez" ("Touch") and "Simon dit" ("Simon says") or "Simon le Simple dit" ("Simple Simon says").
2) The teacher chooses a body part or item of clothing and states, "Touchez" or "Simon dit, 'Touchez.' " (Ex. "Touchez la tête," or "Simon dit, 'Touchez la tête.' ")
3) The children may touch the appropriate body part or item of clothing only if Simon has given them permission.
4) The teacher checks to see if the children have responded correctly. If they are having trouble, visual cues may be used. (Ex. pointing to the appropriate part of the body.)

VARIATIONS:

1) The teacher may call on children individually, becoming increasingly insistent, to see if the children really understand. (Ex. The teacher may say in a firm voice, "Anna, touche la tête!" The command may be repeated to Anna several times, in various tones of voice.)
2) After practice, one of the children may become the leader and issue the commands.

EXTENSIONS:

1) New command verbs may be added. (Ex. "Asseyez-vous," 'Levez-vous," "Ouvrez," and "Fermez.")
2) "Oui" and "non" may be introduced as well, so that the children can respond to the commands both verbally and physically.

POINTS OF INTEREST:

1) Controlling when to move and when not to move the body.
2) Responding correctly to the tricks of the leader.
3) Playing a group game.

DESIGN CUES:

All the children can easily see each other's answers. They therefore have continuous feedback as to the correctness of their response.

TITLE: Commands Grab Bag

PREPARATION: Familiarity with body parts and clothing vocabulary
Familiarity with command verbs

AIMS: To review full sentences using command verbs

MATERIALS:

1) One small bag.
2) Small cards, each containing a written command, or a picture of a person carrying out such a command. (Ex. "Touchez la tête," "Fermez les yeux," etc.)

PRESENTATION:

1) The children sit in a circle.
2) The teacher holds the bag full of cards and asks the child to reach his hand in and choose one card.
3) The teacher reads the command and the child carries it out. The child must hold this new position throughout the game.
4) Each child has a turn. The teacher then returns to the first child and goes around the circle again. This time the children must hold the first position while also carrying out the new command. (Ex. Touching one's head and opening one's mouth at the same time.)
5) The game is over when all the cards have been chosen.

VARIATIONS:

1) Two or three children may be given the same command at once.
2) The child may carry out his action on the next child in line. (Ex. In response to "Touchez la tête," the child may touch his neighbor's head.)
3) One child may be a leader (when picture cards are used), and issue the commands.
4) The child may state aloud the command that he has chosen, and then perform the appropriate action.

EXTENSIONS:

After the written word is introduced, the children may read aloud the written commands.

POINTS OF INTEREST:

1) The physical action involved in holding the various positions.
2) The interest in watching others hold amusing positions.

TITLE: Story: "The Red Balloon" plus color learning

PREPARATION: Assumes no previous knowledge

AIMS:

1) To introduce color vocabulary.
2) To familiarize the children with the life of a young boy in France.

MATERIALS: Balloons of varying colors

PRESENTATION:

1) "The Red Balloon," by Albert Lamorisse is read to the children (see Appendix D).
2) The children are taught the color "rouge" ("red").
3) The children are then each given a balloon, and taught to say the color of their own balloon.

VARIATIONS:

Children may eventually be taught the colors of other children's balloons.

EXTENSIONS:

1) Children may be taught the words "le ballon" (balloon) and eventually pair this word with the different color adjectives (ex. "le ballon rouge").
2) Children may practice writing the color of their balloon after the written word has been introduced.
3) The movie of "The Red Balloon" may be shown.

POINTS OF INTEREST:

1) Listening to an exciting story.
2) Owning a balloon.

TITLE: I Spy Game

PREPARATION: Familiarity with color vocabulary

AIMS: To review color vocabulary

MATERIALS: A room filled with colorful objects

PRESENTATION:

1) The teacher looks around the room and then states, "I spy with my magic eye, something that is . . ." She then names a color of an object in the room (ex. "rouge," "jaune," "bleu," etc.).
2) The children take turns trying to guess which object the teacher is speaking about.
3) This is repeated until all the children have had at least one turn.

VARIATIONS:

After one child has guessed the correct object, he or she then becomes the leader and "spies" something in the room.

EXTENSIONS:

1) Children learn the names of the different objects set out in the room and eventually hear these names paired with the appropriate color adjective (ex. "I spy with my magic eye, 'la porte rouge' ").
2) Other adjectives may eventually be used: for example, "grand" ("big"), "petit" ("little"), and the numbers.
3) Eventually, the entire "I spy" statement may be posed to the children in French. First "je vois" may be presented, later "avec mon oeil magique," and finally "quelque chose qui est . . . ," and so on.

POINTS OF INTEREST:

1) Searching for the object.
2) Trying to find "tricky" objects.

TITLE: Apple Coloring

PREPARATION: Knowledge of several colors

AIMS:

1) To introduce new color vocabulary.
2) To review previously learned color vocabulary.

MATERIALS:

1) Drawing paper.
2) Crayons for colors chosen.

PRESENTATION:

1) In the fall, when apples are abundant, different colored apples may be brought in and shown to the children. (Ex. red, green, yellow.)
2) The corresponding French terms are presented to the children.
3) Children may repeat the new vocabulary, and then color in pictures of the different kinds of apples.

VARIATIONS:

The teacher may choose only one color to focus on, if need be, instead of all three.

EXTENSIONS:

1) The instructor may bring in other fruits and vegetables of different colors (ex. oranges, bananas, peppers) to further expand the color vocabulary.
2) The teacher may introduce the word "le pomme" and pair it with the various color adjectives. (Ex. "le pomme rouge," "le pomme jaune," etc.)
3) When the children have begun to read, the teacher may present name cards for the colors, and have them match the name cards to the appropriate apples.
4) The children may eventually copy the color words underneath the corresponding apple drawings.

POINTS OF INTEREST

1) Handling the various fruits and vegetables.
2) Coloring the drawings to match the objects.

TITLE: Flag Coloring

PREPARATION:

1) Familiarity with the concept of countries (the teacher may give a brief talk on this subject).
2) Explanation of what a flag is.

AIMS:

1) To become familiar with the French flag.
2) To learn or review the three colors: "rouge," "bleu," and "blanc."

MATERIALS:

1) A French flag or picture of a French flag.
2) A red, a white, and a blue crayon for each child.
3) A dittoed copy of a French flag (not colored) for each child.

PRESENTATION:

1) The teacher explains that each country has a flag, what a flag is for, and so on.
2) The French flag is then presented to the children.
3) Each color in the flag is pronounced for them.
4) The children repeat the colors and then color in their picture appropriately.

VARIATIONS:

The children may ask for the appropriate crayons (in French).

EXTENSIONS:

1) The children may learn to write the color names on the flag ditto and may also practice reading these names.
2) For older children, flags may be made either by gluing or sewing fabric.

POINTS OF INTEREST:

1) The joy of coloring.
2) The thrill of holding and looking at the flag.

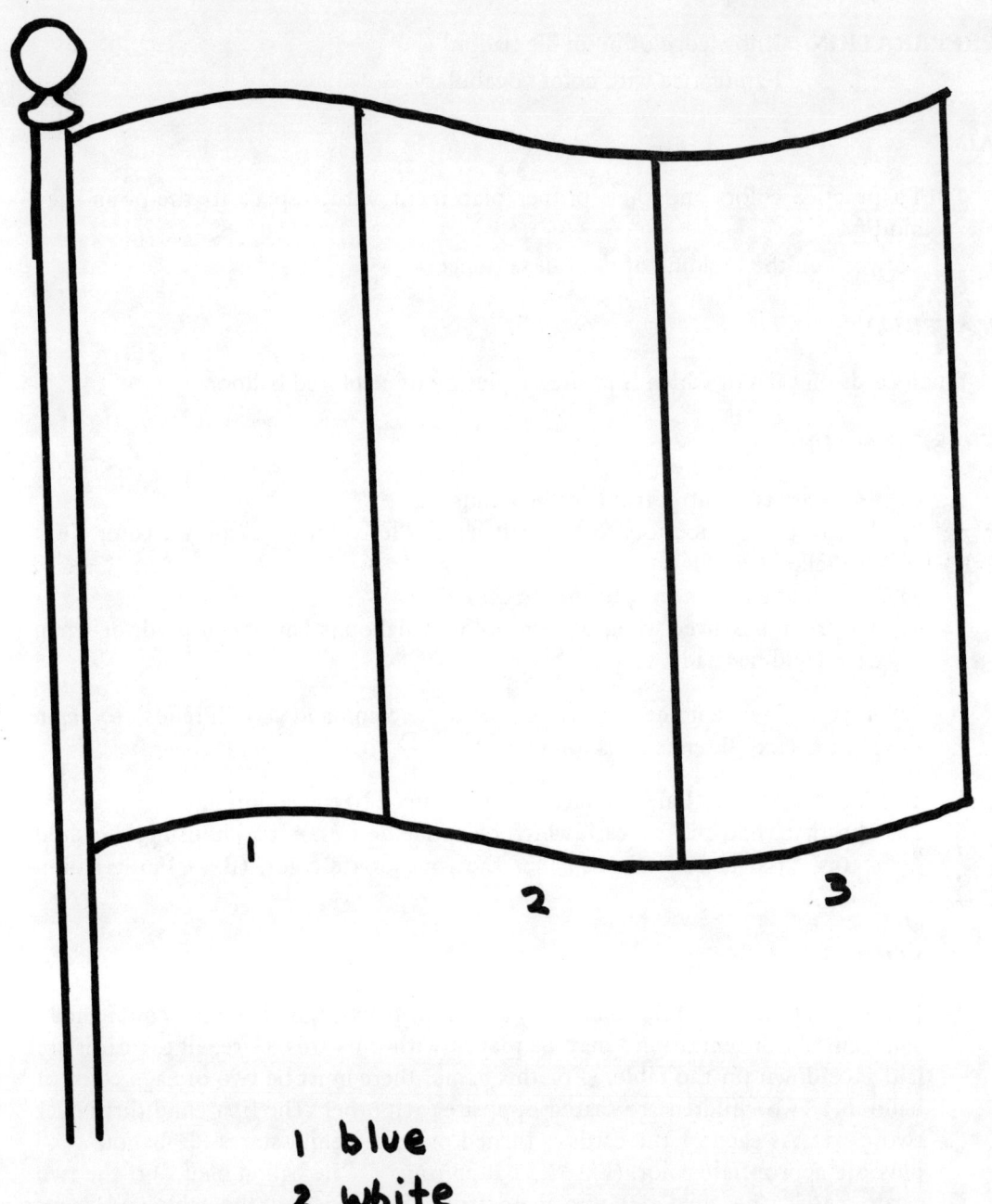

1 blue
2 white
3 red

TITLE: Balloon Card Game

PREPARATION: Knowledge of noun "le ballon"
Familiarity with color vocabulary

AIMS:

1) To practice colors and their proper placement with respect to the noun they modify.
2) To work on the building of the full sentence.

MATERIALS:

Small cards on each of which is printed a picture of a colored balloon.

PRESENTATION:

A. 1) Cards are laid out in front of the children.
   2) The teacher announces to the first child, "le ballon . . ." plus a color. (Ex. "le ballon vert.")
   3) The child chooses an appropriate card.
   4) The round is over when all the colored balloons have been used, or when each child has had a turn.

B. Same as "A," except the teacher now uses the command verb "Prends" to begin the phrase. (Ex. "Prends le ballon vert.")

C. 1) The expression "J'ai," "I have," is introduced to the children.
   2) The first child picks a card which he or she desires. After choosing, the child states, "J'ai le ballon . . ." plus the appropriate color. (Ex. "J'ai le ballon vert.")

VARIATIONS:

1) In presentations A and B, a child may act as the teacher and issue the commands.
2) The game "Concentration" may be played with the cards. Here, all the cards are laid face down on the table. (For this game, there must be two of each color of balloon.) Two children are seated opposite each other. The first child turns over two cards. As each of the cards is turned over, the child states "le ballon . . ." plus the appropriate color. (Ex. "Le ballon rouge," "Le ballon bleu.") If the two cards match, the child removes them from their place at the table and keeps them until the end of the game. If they do not match, they are once again turned face down in their original places. The winner is the person with the most cards. This variation is good for work without the teacher.

EXTENSIONS:

1) The teacher may introduce the verb "rendre" and have the children hand back as well as take the appropriate cards, for Presentation B.
2) When the children have learned the numbers, the teacher may introduce the word "Combien?" and pose questions such as, "Combien de ballons rouges y a-t-il?"
3) Presentations A or B may be recorded on tape with time allotted for the child to choose the appropriate card. The child may check his answer by listening to the tape. For example, after the child has chosen, the tape might say, "Did you choose the red balloon? Then you are right." Earphones may be provided so that the children can work individually.
4) The teacher may make up two stacks of cards, one containing numbers, the other containing the colored balloons. The child turns over one card from each pile and then forms a sentence using the number plus the noun plus the adjective, such as, "Cinq ballons rouges."

POINTS OF INTEREST:

1) Looking at and working with the brightly colored balloon pictures.
2) Remembering the story about the balloons which was read earlier.

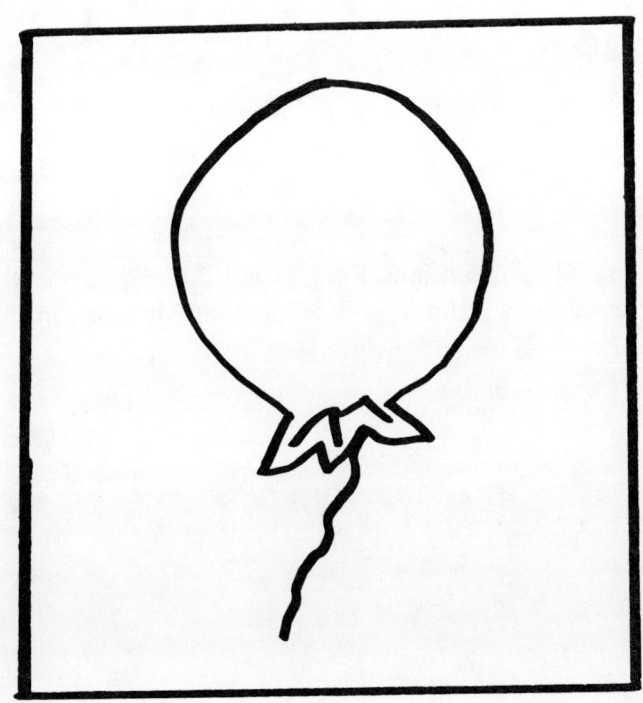

TITLE: Color Bingo

PREPARATION: Familiarity with body parts and clothing vocabulary
Familiarity with colors

AIMS:

1) To work on the proper placement of adjectives with respect to the nouns they modify.
2) To review past vocabulary.

MATERIALS:

1) One "bingo" game card for every child in the group. A card is divided into three rows of three squares each. Within each square is a picture of one of the body parts, every one a different color. (Ex. The child's card might contain a picture of blue eyes in one square, red eyes in another, a blue foot in another, and so on.)
2) Bingo markers.
3) Individual cards with the same pictures that are drawn on the bingo cards. These "draw pile" cards should contain only one picture per card.

PRESENTATION AND VARIATIONS: See Bingo

POINTS OF INTEREST:

1) Playing a more challenging version of a familiar game.
2) Looking at the familiar, but more colorful pictures.

DESIGN CUES:

Children are exposed to repetition of words and pictures similar to those found in Bingo. The old vocabulary is thus reinforced in a slightly new context.

TITLE: Magic Clothesline Game

PREPARATION: Familiarity with body parts and clothing vocabulary
Familiarity with color vocabulary
Familiarity with the command verb "Prends" ("Take")

AIMS:

1) To practice using verbs and forming meaningful sentences.
2) To emphasize the proper placement of nouns and adjectives in the sentence.
3) To review previously learned vocabulary.

MATERIALS:

1) One large string that may be attached to two different points in the room, so that a large "clothesline" is formed.
2) Cards (at least one per child) showing pictures of the colored body parts. There should be one body part per card. (Examples are cards with red eyes, an orange leg, a green arm, and so on.) Taped to the back of each card is a paper clip which is bent so that the cards may be hung on the "clothesline."

PRESENTATION:

A. 1) All the cards are hung on the clothesline. The children are seated so that they may see the cards.
   2) The teacher addresses the first child in a manner such as the following: "Jason, prends la chemise bleu."
   3) The child walks over to the clothesline and chooses the corresponding card.
   4) The game is over when all the cards have been chosen.

B. After the children have mastered Presentation A, each child may choose a card from the clothesline. After choosing, the child states, "J'ai" plus the description of the object chosen. (Ex. "J'ai les pantalons verts.")

VARIATIONS:

1) The teacher instructs the children to close their eyes. One card from the clothesline is then removed. The children open their eyes and try to guess what is missing.
2) One child takes the role of the teacher and issues the commands.

EXTENSIONS:

After the written word is introduced, each child may be given a written word card describing one object on the clothesline. The child must read the card and then hang it next to the appropriate body part or item of clothing already on the line.

POINTS OF INTEREST:

1) Seeing the brightly colored pictures on the clothesline.
2) Choosing a favorite body part or item of clothing or one that is a favorite color.

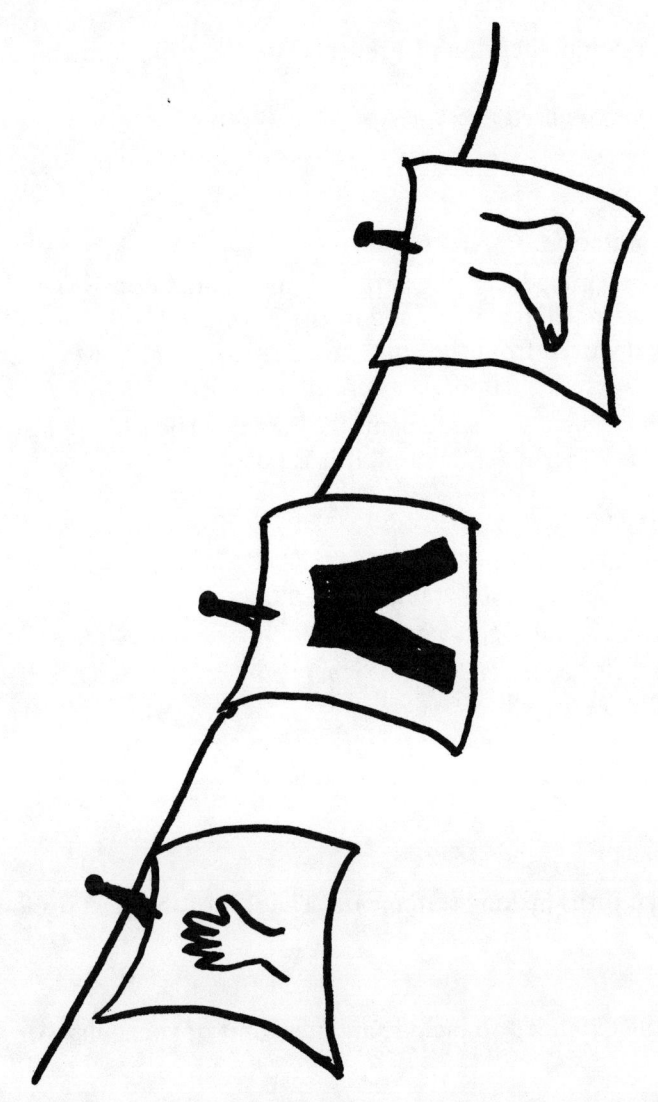

TITLE: "Oui ou Non" Word Game

PREPARATION:

1) Familiarity with words "oui" ("yes") and "non" ("no").
2) For Presentation A: familiarity with the *body part plus color* construction.
3) For Presentation B: familiarity with the *number plus body part* construction.
4) For Presentation C: familiarity with the *number plus body part plus color* construction.
5) For Presentation D: familiarity with the *number plus family member* construction.

AIMS: To practice comprehension of French sentences using known vocabulary.

MATERIALS: None required

PRESENTATION

1) General Presentation:
   a) The teacher introduces the words "oui" and "non" to the children. No explanation need be given about the forms "Il a," "elle a," etc. as these are easily deduced from the context. (Gesticulation, however, such as pointing to the person talked about, is a very useful aid.)
   b) The teacher makes a statement in French. The children are instructed to say "oui" if it is true, and "non" if it is false.

2) Sample Statements:
   a) *Presentation A; Body part plus color*: "Jason a les yeux bleus. Oui ou non?," "Anna a les pieds oranges. Oui ou non?"
   b) *Presentation B; Body part plus number*: "Erika a deux têtes. Oui ou non?"
   c) *Presentation C; Number plus Body part plus color*: "Sarah a deux bras rouges. Oui ou non?"
   d) Presentation D; Number *plus family member*: "Dana a cinq pères. Oui ou non?" "Michael a deux frères. Oui ou non?"

VARIATIONS:

The children take turns making statements. The rest of the class responds.

EXTENSIONS:

This game may be extended to include any new unit of vocabulary or grammar.

POINTS OF INTEREST:

1) Comprehending the often amusing statements.
2) Evaluating the truth of the statements.

DESIGN CUES:

The children are obliged to evaluate the truth of the statement. They must therefore listen attentively and comprehend the sentence in its entirety before they can make a sound judgment.

TITLE: Number Bingo

PREPARATION: Familiarity with the French names for the numerals "1-5" and later "6-10"

AIMS: To practice the French names for these numerals

MATERIALS:

1) One "bingo" game card for every child in the group. A card is divided into three rows of three squares each. Within each square is written a numeral from 1-10.
2) Bingo markers to place on the squares.
3) "Draw pile" cards with a numeral from "1-10" printed on each card.

PRESENTATION:

1) Each child is given a card and some markers.
2) The teacher chooses a card from the draw pile and announces, in French, the numeral written on that card.
3) The children look for the corresponding numeral on their own cards. If they find it, they place a marker on the appropriate number.
4) The game is over when one child fills up all the spaces on his or her card.

VARIATIONS:

1) The game may be over when one child has three markers lined up in a row (horizontally, diagonally, or vertically).
2) After practice, one child may be the leader and announce the numerals on the cards from the draw pile, while the other children play as before.

EXTENSIONS:

1) After the written word is introduced, the written words for the numbers may be substituted for the numerals on the game cards and draw pile cards. The children must now read the words in order to know where to place the markers.
2) For individual work, no markers need be used. The draw pile cards may contain the written number words, while the game cards may contain only the numerals. The child must then match the words from the draw pile to the appropriate numerals on the game cards. If a method for self-correction is desired, the draw pile cards may also have their numerals printed on the back. In this way, when the child is finished matching the words of the draw pile to the numerals on the game card, he may then turn the draw cards over and check to see if they match the numeral of the game card.

POINTS OF INTEREST:

1) Working with numbers.
2) Placing the markers on the numbers.
3) Using a familiar game in a new context.
4) Playing a game with other children.

DESIGN CUES:

1) Due to prior familiarity with numerals, the child can easily assume the role of the leader in Variation 2.
2) Methods such as Extension 2 may be devised so that the child may work individually and check what he has done.

TITLE: Numerical Grab Bag

PREPARATION: Familiarity with the Commands Grab Bag Game (see page 26)

MATERIALS:

1) Materials used in the Commands Grab Bag Game.
2) A second small bag, preferably of a different color.
3) Small cards, each one with a numeral written on one side (the teacher may begin with "1-5" and later add "6-10").

PRESENTATION:

1) The children sit in a circle.
2) The teacher holds the first bag full of command cards and asks a child to reach his hand in and choose one card.
3) The teacher reads the card aloud.
4) The teacher then picks up the second grab bag, and has a second child choose a number card.
5) The teacher states in French the number that appears on the card.
6) The children must repeat the first action (drawn from the commands grab bag) for the number of times stated on the number card. (Ex. Opening one's eyes five times.)
7) The teacher counts out loud with the children as everyone executes the commands.

VARIATIONS:

1) The children may execute the commands one at a time.
2) A child may carry out his action on the next child in line. (Ex. He may touch his neighbor's head 6 times.)
3) One child may be the leader and issue the commands.
4) One child may state aloud the command that he has chosen, and then perform the appropriate action.

EXTENSIONS:

1) New activity words may be introduced (ex. "sauter," "to jump," "tourner," "to turn," "applaudir," "to clap," and so on).
2) After the written word is introduced, the commands as well as the numbers should be written out in words. The children may then read aloud the words on the cards.

POINTS OF INTEREST:

1) Repeating the actions over and over again.
2) The suspense involved in putting together the two messages from the different bags.
3) Playing a familiar game in a new and amusing fashion.
4) Counting and watching.

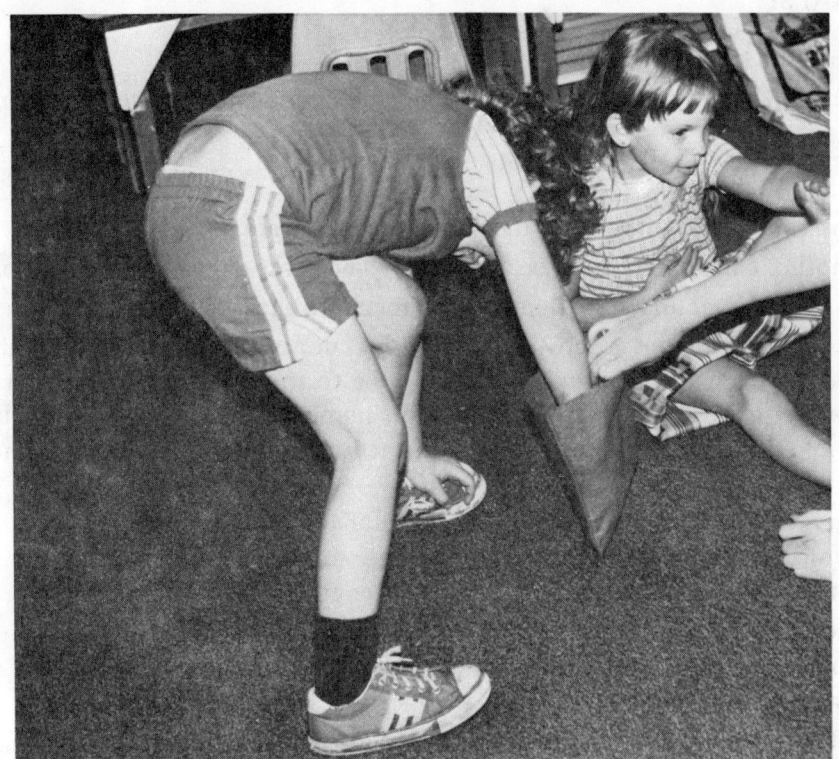

TITLE: Rhythm Chants and Body Movement (Indian Chief)

PREPARATION: Familiarity with numbers: first, 1-5, later 1-10

AIMS:

1) To review number vocabulary
2) To work with counting

MATERIALS:

1) One grab bag (approximately 5" x 9")
2) Strips of paper with the numbers "1-5" and later "1-10" written on them

PRESENTATION:

1) One child is chosen to leave the room; the others are seated in a circle.
2) Another child is chosen to be the "chief" and picks a number from the bag.
3) This child announces the number, in French, to the other members of the group.
4) The chief leads the group through varying motions; clapping, tapping the floor, shaking fingers, and so on. These are done to the count of the number chosen. For example, if the child has chosen the number three, he or she may clap three times, then tap the floor three times, then touch the shoulders three times, and so on.
5) The group copies the chief, and all count out loud together. In the above example, the children would chant, "un-deux-trois, un-deux-trois!" as they carried out the motions, changing their action after every three counts.
6) The absented child reenters the room, and after watching the group for a few moments, tries to guess who the chicf is. This child may be given two or three chances to guess correctly.
7) After the guesses, the real chief leaves the room, a new chief is chosen, and the game is repeated.

VARIATIONS:

If the children are having trouble following the counts, the game may be played without having someone leaving the room and trying to guess. In other words, one child may choose a number from the grab bag, and the entire group may practice the various rhythms together.

POINTS OF INTEREST:

1) Guessing who the chief is.
2) Inventing interesting motions.
3) Chanting rhythmically as a group.

TITLE: How Many?

PREPARATION: Familiarity with number vocabulary: first numbers 1-5, later numbers 1-10

AIMS:

1) To learn and practice counting and quantity.
2) To later respond to questions about quantity.
3) To eventually place a number next to a familiar noun.
4) To eventually work on forming full sentences.

MATERIALS:

1) *For Presentation A:* 10 pennies, buttons, or anything that the child has not yet learned the French word for.
2) *For Presentation B, C, and D:* several sets of 10 cards each. Every set should contain one picture on each card, all of the same object. The pictures should be of something the child has learned to say in French; for example, 10 balloons, 10 heads, 10 feet, and so on.

PRESENTATION:

A. 1) A certain number of objects is placed before the child. The child is instructed to count them aloud, and to announce how many there are. (Later, the counting may be dispensed with, and the child may state only the quantity present.)
2) The teacher adds or takes away several objects. The next child counts them and states how many there are. The game is over when each child has had a turn to count.
3) The teacher, of course, does not present all ten numbers in the beginning. He or she may first deal with only five objects; later 10, and then perhaps up to 20, depending upon the interest of the children.

B. Same as A, except the familiar picture cards are substituted for the objects.

C. 1) The question "Combien?" is introduced. Children are told that "Combien" means "How many?" The teacher then asks, "Combien de _____ y a-t-il?" (The blank is filled in with the noun represented by the picture card set. For example, Combien de têtes y a-t-il?")
2) The teacher proceeds as in A and B.
3) Eventually different sets of picture cards are used.

D. Same as C, except this time, after the children count, they must answer in the *number plus noun* form; ex. "cinq ballons," "six têtes," and so on.

E. The children may eventually add the phrase "il y a" to form full sentences. (Ex. "Il y a cinq ballons.")

VARIATIONS:

The child may eventually ask the question beginning with "combien?"

EXTENSIONS:

1) The teacher may introduce the verb "prendre" and state, "Prends deux," "Prends deux," "Prends cinq" and so on.
2) Later the teacher may lay out all the sets of cards in front of the children (or perhaps, in the beginning only four cards from each set. The children may then be asked for a certain amount of each item. (Ex. "Erika, prends six ballons" or "Michael, prends trois chemises.")
3) Later, different commands may be added, such as orders beginning with "rends" ("hand back"), "Donne-moi" ("give me"), and so on.
4) The children can count in French with the number rods, spindle boxes, or other math materials.

POINTS OF INTEREST:

1) Counting in a foreign language.
2) Finding the proper quantity and presenting it to the teacher.
3) Manipulating cards and objects.

TITLE: Monster Game

PREPARATION:

1) Familiarity with body parts vocabulary
2) Familiarity with colors vocabulary
3) Familiarity with numbers (at least "1-5")
4) Familiarity with "j'ai" ("I have")

AIMS:

1) To practice the proper placement of adjectives in the sentences.
2) To review past vocabulary.

MATERIALS:

A set of cards (at least one or two cards per child), each printed with the picture of a different "monster." A typical "monster" might have three heads, five blue eyes and one foot; or one red nose, three arms, and so on.

PRESENTATION:

A. Recognition
   1) All the cards are laid out in front of the children.
   2) The teacher pretends to be one of the monsters. Disguising his or her voice, the instructor addresses the first child and describes the monster's appearance. (Ex. "J'ai la chemise bleu, j'ai trois têtes, et j'ai cinq yeux verts.")
   3) The child must select the card with the appropriate monster.
   4) The teacher addresses the second child, disguising his or her voice differently this time, and giving the description of another monster.
   5) The game is over when all the cards have been played.

B. Production

   The child must choose a monster card and must speak for that monster, starting with "J'ai . . ." The child may disguise his or her voice if so desired.

VARIATIONS:

One child may act as the teacher and speak for a monster. Other children in turn try to choose the correct monster card.

Some Sample Monsters:
Sample Descriptions:

① J'ai le nez rouge

② J'ai deux têtes, j'ai la chemise jaune, et j'ai les pantalons verts

③ J'ai quatre bras. J'ai la main rouge, j'ai la main verte, j'ai la main bleue, et j'ai la main jaune.

④ J'ai trois yeux rouges.

EXTENSIONS:

1) After the children have mastered Presentations A and B, they may be given the outline of a monster face. The teacher dictates a short description of a monster she is pretending to be. (Ex. "J'ai le nez rouge," or "J'ai deux yeux bleus.") With the aid of crayons, the children color their monster faces accordingly.

2) If the children wish to work individually, the teacher may make a tape of the different monster descriptions, allotting time after each one, so that the child may choose the appropriate monster card. As a means of self-correction, each monster card could be numbered, and after the child has picked the card, the tape could announce which number card should have been chosen.
Ex. Tape of Monster: J'ai la chemise bleu.
   (Space allotted so that the child may choose. The child chooses monster card 2.)
Ex. Tape of Monster: Did you choose card 2? That is the answer. I am the monster with the blue shirt.
Naturally, the children must be instructed in the proper use of the tape recorder, and earphones may be provided so that they may work without disturbing others.

3) After the written word is introduced, the teacher may make a separate set of cards with written descriptions of the monsters. Children may then read the cards and match them to the appropriate monster cards. Matching cards could have matching numbers or designs printed on the back, so that the child may check his or her own work.

POINTS OF INTEREST:

1) Seeing the amusing pictures of the monsters.
2) Disguising one's voice to speak like monsters.
3) Choosing one's own monster; pretending to be the monster of one's choice.

DESIGN CUES:

1) The child must work on forming coherent and accurate sentences.
2) In Extensions 2 and 3, matching numbers or designs helps provide corrective feedback.

TITLE: Number plus noun plus color book

PREPARATION: Familiarity with number, noun, and color vocabulary

AIMS:

1) Introduction of the written word.
2) Review of the placement of adjectives with respect to the nouns they modify.
3) Review of previously learned vocabulary.

MATERIALS:

A book, approximately 5" x 9", which is constructed in the following manner:

On each page is written a number from one to ten. The number should be written in the upper left hand corner and lower right hand corner of the page. In the center of the page, a picture of that quantity of an object is drawn. For example, if the number is one, a picture of one object is drawn in the center of the page. The object should be something that the children have learned the French word for. The French description of the object and its quantity are written below the picture. There should be ten pages to the book, each representing a number from one to ten, and arranged in order starting from number 1. Our number book contained the following pages:

1) un nez rouge
2) deux mains jaunes
3) trois chemises bleus
4) quatre amis
5) cinq yeux verts
6) six têtes oranges
7) sept pieds rouges
8) huit pantalons
9) neuf ballons
10) dix bouches rouges

Ex.

PRESENTATION:

1) The teacher turns to the first page of the book and asks if anyone can name in French the number printed on the page.
2) The teacher then reads the French words written on the page, while showing the children the accompanying picture. The children are asked for an English translation.
3) The teacher and the children repeat the French words together. The teacher then turns the page and repeats the sequence.

VARIATIONS:

1) The teacher may ask the children to guess in French what the words say (this is not too difficult due to the clarity of the pictures).
2) After practice, one child may read the book to the teacher or to the other children.

EXTENSIONS:

1) Children may draw their own copy of the book or make up a different number book.
2) A new number book with written words and no numerals may be devised so that the child must concentrate more on reading.

POINTS OF INTEREST:

1) Reading French words for the first time.
2) Looking at the amusing pictures found in the book.

DESIGN CUES:

1) The pictures aid the children in recognition of the words written.
2) The pictures provide an additional image which can aid in remembering the numbers.

TITLE: What's Your Name?

PREPARATION: Children are taught "je m'appelle" ("My name is") and "Comment t'appelles-tu?" ("What's your name?")

AIMS: To practice the above vocabulary

MATERIALS: 1 soda bottle

PRESENTATION:

1) Children are seated in a circle. The bottle is placed in the center on its side.
2) The teacher spins the bottle. The neck of the bottle points to one person in the circle.
3) The teacher poses the question "Comment t'appelles-tu?" to this person.
4) The child responds "Je m'appelle" plus his or her name. (Ex. "Je m'appelle Sarah.")

VARIATIONS:

Children may spin the bottle and practice asking questions and giving answers.

EXTENSIONS:

1) When the family members unit is completed, questions such as the following may be posed: "Ta mère, comment s'appelle-t-elle?" "Ta soeur, comment s'appelle-t-elle?," and so on.
2) The teacher may ask different kinds of questions to the child the bottle points to. For example, the instructor might point to another member of the group and ask the child, "Comment s'appelle-t-il?" or "Comment s'appelle-t-elle?" The child may simply respond with the appropriate name (ex. "Mary" or "Alex") or may eventually be taught "Il s'appelle," "Elle s'appelle," "Tu t'appelles," and so on.
3) This game may be extended to other units as well. Questions about numbers, colors, or body parts may be asked of the child to whom the bottle points. The teacher may also use this game in conjunction with activities such as the commands grab bag; the person whom the bottle points to must choose a card from the bag.

POINTS OF INTEREST:

1) Watching and making the bottle spin.
2) Listening to the variety of questions asked.
3) Waiting to see who the bottle will land on.

TITLE: Family Coloring

PREPARATION: Assumes no previous knowledge

MATERIALS:

1) Drawing paper.
2) Crayons

PRESENTATION:

1) The teacher presents the words "Ma mère" ("my mother"), "mon père" ("my father"), "ma soeur" ("my sister"), and "mon frère" ("my brother"), stressing any French-English word similarities.
2) The children are instructed to first draw a picture of their mother and to repeat the words "ma mère."
3) After the children have finished their drawing, the class draws a second family member, proceeding exactly as before.

VARIATIONS:

The children may present their drawings, explaining (in French) who is who in their pictures.

EXTENSIONS:

The written words may eventually be presented to the children so that they can label their drawings appropriately.

POINTS OF INTEREST:

1) Coloring one's own family.
2) Presenting one's family picture to the class.

TITLE: Family Pantomime Game

PREPARATION: Knowledge of family members vocabulary

AIMS: To review the above vocabulary

MATERIALS: None required

PRESENTATION: (This game is best played in small groups of about 3-4 children.)

1) The teacher reviews the family members vocabulary with the children.
2) The teacher then asks each child to name one thing each member of his or her family likes to do. Sample responses were, "My father likes to read the paper," "My mother likes to jog," "My brother likes to tease me," and "My sister likes to tickle me."
3) After the teacher listens to all the responses, he or she acts out the activity of one member of somebody's family. If a child recognizes the action as being one of the pastimes of someone in his or her family, the child calls out in French the person whom the teacher is imitating. (Ex. The teacher starts to jog around the room. One child recognizes the action and calls out "ma mère.")

VARIATIONS:

1) One child may do the pantomiming while the others guess.
2) If the children are having difficulty remembering all the vocabulary at once, only one family member may be dealt with at a time. In other words, a review of the expression "ma mère" might be given and the pantomimes of all the mothers presented. Then a review of "mon père" might be given, and the pantomimes of the fathers demonstrated. All the family members might be dealt with in this way.

EXTENSIONS:

1) A "grab bag" might be devised with each of the family members names printed on strips of paper to be placed in the bag. The child must choose a card and act out the family member chosen, while the others try to guess who it is.
2) When the written word is introduced, children may be given a French word card for each member of their family. When they see the appropriate pantomime, the children may state the correct family member expression and hold up the corresponding word card.

POINTS OF INTEREST:

1) Watching the pantomimes of someone in the child's own family.
2) Distinguishing which child the pantomime belongs to.
3) Remembering the appropriate French word.

TITLE: Family plus Adjective Card Game

PREPARATION:

1) Familiarity with family vocabulary
2) Familiarity with color adjectives
3) Familiarity with "Prends" and "J'ai"
4) Familiarity with numbers

AIMS:

1) To work on using family member nouns with an adjective (and, in a sense, to see that adjectives may be added to any noun).
2) To practice using and recognizing full sentences with the verb forms "Prends" and "J'ai."
3) To review previously learned vocabulary.

MATERIALS:

A set of cards (about 20), each of which contains a picture of a family member (mother, father, brother, or sister). There should therefore be 5 pictures of each family member. Within each family member category, some of the 5 pictures are colored one color, and the rest are another color. Example: There might be 3 yellow mothers, 2 red mothers, 1 blue father, 4 green fathers, 5 orange brothers, 4 red sisters, and 1 orange sister.

PRESENTATION:

A. Recognition
1) All the cards are laid out in front of the children.
2) The teacher addresses the first child and says, "Prends plus number plus family member plus color." Example: "Dana, prends deux mères rouges."
3) The child listens to the instructions and takes the appropriate cards.
4) The teacher continues in this manner until all the cards are used up.

B. Production
1) All the cards are laid out in front of the children.
2) The child chooses one subset of cards (one color of a family member) and says "J'ai plus the number plus the family member plus the color." Ex.: "J'ai trois mères rouges."

VARIATIONS:

1) Cards which are not colored may be made for each family member. In this way, a simpler version of the game may be played, in which the teacher asks only "Prends plus number plus family member." Example: "Prends deux mères." For Presentation B, the child may take two brothers and say "J'ai deux freres," and so on.

2) For Presentation A, Recognition, the child may act as the teacher and issue the commands.

EXTENSIONS:

1) Verbs such as "rendre" ("to hand in") and "Donne-moi" ("give me") may be introduced, and the game played as in Presentation A.

2) New adjectives may be taught to the children (ex. "Heureux," "heureuse" ("happy"), "triste" ("sad"), "fâché," "fachée" ("angry"), and so on. An appropriate set of cards may be made, eliminating the colors and substituting facial expressions depicting the new set of adjectives. The game may then be played as before, using the new adjectives instead of the colors.

3) After the written word is introduced, cards may be made up with written commands or descriptions on them. Ex.: "Prends un père jaune," or simply "un père jaune." The children may match the written descriptions to the appropriate picture cards. A self-correction system may be developed so that numbers on the backs of each of the two sets of cards are the same when a correct match has been made. In this way, the children may work individually and check their own work.

POINTS OF INTEREST:

1) Choosing the attractively drawn cards.
2) Looking at the colored family members and the pictures with the amusing facial expressions.
3) Doing a somewhat involved and challenging exercise.

TITLE: Food Card Game

PREPARATION:

Introduction of French terms for the foods to be learned and those to be consumed at the tea party. (We chose "le pain" ("bread"), "le beurre" ("butter"), "le chocolat" ("chocolate"), "le lait" ("milk"), and "le thé" ("tea").

AIMS:

1) To have the children recognize and eventually reproduce the food vocabulary.
2) To understand and use a command plus the food vocabulary, and to learn to say "Please" and "Thank you."
3) To use the food vocabulary with a first person conjugated verb, namely "J'ai."

MATERIALS:

A set of cards, on each card of which is drawn a picture of one of the foods to be learned.

PRESENTATION:

A. 1) Children review the food vocabulary with the teacher.
   2) The cards are spread out in front of the children.
   3) The teacher addresses one child and names one of the foods. Ex. "le chocolat."
   4) The child must find the appropriate card and present it to the teacher.
   5) The teacher names another food for the next child, and so on.

B. 1) The teacher introduces the phrases "Passez-moi" or "Passe-moi" ("Pass me"), "S'il vous plaît" or "S'il te plaît" ("Please"), and "merci" ("thank you"). The instructor gives the translation for these words and discusses the reason for their use.
   2) The game proceeds as in A, except this time the teacher says "Passe-moi" (or "Passez-moi") plus the food plus S'il te plaît (or "S'il vous plaît"). After the child gives the teacher the appropriate card, the teacher says, "Merci." (Ex. "Passe moi le beurre, s'il te plaît." The child passes it. "Merci.")

C. The children in turn pick the card they desire. After they choose their card, they are instructed to state, "J'ai" plus the food they have chosen. (Ex. "J'ai le beurre.")

D. Multiple cards for each food may be made up and set out before the children. The child must then choose several cards of one food and use the construction "J'ai plus number plus noun" to describe how many he has. (Ex. "J'ai cinq chocolats.")

EXTENSIONS:

1) Later, after the written word is introduced, descriptions of the foods may be written right below the pictures on the cards. After, the written words may be detached from the picture cards, and both words and pictures may be mixed up and placed before the child. Then, when the teacher asks the child for "le chocolat," for example, the child must hand in both the picture card and the written word card for "le chocolat."

2) A tape recording may be made of the teacher asking for foods, with time allotted for the children to choose the cards. After the child has chosen, the tape might say, for example, "Did you choose the butter? Then you are right!" In this way, the children may work individually. Earphones may be used, and children should be instructed in the proper use of the tape recorder.

POINTS OF INTEREST:

1) Looking at attractive pictures of familiar foods.
2) Discovering which card is being talked about.
3) Hearing (and later saying) "merci" when the child has given the teacher the correct word.

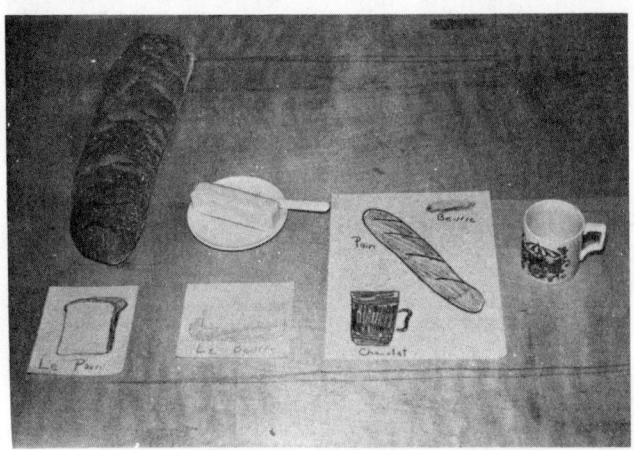

TITLE: French Tea Party

PREPARATION: Familiarity with the food vocabulary and table expressions presented in the Food Card Game

AIMS:

1) To practice the above vocabulary in a real life and enjoyable situation.
2) To experience certain French customs.

MATERIALS:

1) Everything to be served at the tea party (see Appendix B). For chocolate, we purchased a special spread called "Nuttela" which may be obtained in some gourmet stores. In this way, we could enjoy the delicious European custom of eating bread and chocolate.
2) Utensils, napkins, plates, cups, etc.

PRESENTATION:

1) The children are instructed to stand at their places at the table. All food and drinks are near the teacher.
2) The teacher explains a little about the foods at the party (ex. about bread and chocolate). The teacher then explains that all speaking will be done in French, and that everyone must pretend not to understand English. The instructor says "Asseyez-vous" and everybody sits down.
3) The teacher gives a demonstration with another teacher or with an older child on how to ask for the food at the table.
   Ex.: Teacher: "Anna, passe-moi le pain, s'il te plaît."
   Anna passes the bread.
   Teacher: "Merci. Passe-moi le beurre, s'il te plaît."
   Anna passes the butter.
   This is repeated for all the foods or drinks at the table.
4) After the demonstration, the children may ask in turn for whatever they wish to try. If no child initiates the asking, the teacher may simply turn to someone, and, holding up the various items, ask "Anna, du pain?," "Jason, du chocolat?," and so on. The teacher may then help the child ask for the desired object.

EXTENSIONS:

1) Children may be taught "J'aime" ("I like") and "Aimes-tu?" ("Do you like?") at this time. Ex. The teacher asks "Aimes-tu le chocolat? Oui ou non?" The child may answer "oui" or "non" and eventually "J'aime le chocolat" or "Je n'aime pas le chocolat."

2) New food vocabulary may be used at a second tea or lunch party. Related expressions such as "verser" ("to pour") and "couper" ("to cut") may also be introduced.

3) After practice, tea party materials may be made easily accessible to the children, so that two-person tea parties (without a teacher) may be set up during the day. A special two-person tea table may be set aside for this purpose. Rules about speaking French, however, must be strictly adhered to.

POINTS OF INTEREST:

1) The formality of the tea party.
2) The thrill of trying new foods.
3) The joy of asking for the foods in a foreign language, and helping friends ask when they are having trouble. This activity was a huge success.

DESIGN CUES:

In order to receive the treats, the children must ask for them properly.

IDEAS FOR EXPANSION

A. Toward an All-Encompassing Program

The program described in the preceding pages is only, as we pointed out earlier, a beginning to what could eventually be developed. One desirable sequel to these activities might consist of an "immersion" program, in which the child is constantly surrounded by the foreign language and is continually hearing natural conversation. It is by this method that the child can fully make use of his absorbent powers.

The first part of any program may progress in a manner similar to what we have described in this manual. Children may deal with basic vocabulary and grammatical construction, work on limited comprehension and production, and get a general feeling for French language and culture. In this way, the introduction of the new material is gradual and does not leave the children feeling confused or overwhelmed. Learning here proceeds step by step, and it is very easy for the child to use the materials presented.

Eventually, after the children are confident with the old work, a bilingual classroom may be established. A separate part of the room is set aside with a small fence around it and door to enter. The child might even be required to present a "passport" to the supervising teacher or child in the area!

Entering this part of the room is like walking into another country. Only French is spoken here. The room is decorated with travel posters and scenes from French-speaking areas of the world; the furniture is arranged to look like a French café with chairs and round, umbrella-shaped tables. The reason for setting apart this area is simple; in this way, many aspects of French life are brought directly into the classrooms and a feeling of "actually" being there is created.

The fence clearly delineates where only French must be spoken. This is a strict rule which is carefully explained to the children. To help enforce this principle, the instructor begins by opening up the region for only a limited period per day and by providing close supervision. Later, as the children become more accustomed to the idea, the area is left available to them all day.

This two-part program, starting from individual exercises and gradually leading up to a bilingual classroom, is ideal for Montessori settings where children typically spend several years in a classroom. For traditional elementary schools, where children normally spend only 1 year together, the idea may be adapted as follows. In this case, a bilingual classroom is set up immediately, although both French and English is used in the French area at first. Gradually more French is spoken than English, until French becomes the sole language of this area. An alternative to this system is to employ a foreign language teacher and open a separate foreign language room which is accessible to children of all grades. In such a situation, less-experienced children may seek help from the teacher or from those more familiar with the materials.

The French region of the classroom is further divided into three subareas. Children may choose an activity from the shelves in any of the subareas, and may work at a table or on the floor on a special working mat. Each child may work independently or with friends. When he is finished, he places his work back on the shelf in the same condition that he found the material.

The first subarea is made up of low shelves filled with culture work: maps, puzzles of France and of Europe, story and picture books, cooking projects that may be done individually and French music in the form of records and tapes (as well as a phonograph, a tape recorder, and earphones so that the children may listen without disturbing others).

The second subarea is composed of a set of shelves devoted to French language activities. Here the grammar and vocabulary materials presented on the previous pages are set out for individual use. New, advanced materials are gradually added to the shelves, so that both simple and more complex work is available.

The third subarea consists of a small Montessori region, which contains duplicates of some of the materials found elsewhere in the classroom. (Non-Montessori teachers may alter this subarea accordingly.) Work here is made up of activities from the practical life area, such as pouring, buttoning, spooning, and so on, as well as exercises from other areas. The color tablets and number materials are ideal for this section, since they may be used in conjunction with the grammar materials that teach color and number vocabulary. All of the work in this area is presented to the children completely in French. This technique is well suited to our purposes, since the children already know how to use these materials from working with them in the English part of the classroom. The child thus hears the French descriptions paired with what is already familiar. Since the new language is used in a meaningful context, the child will eventually begin to absorb and understand it. Informal, formal, masculine, and feminine forms will naturally be picked up, just as they are absorbed by the child who grows up in a French-speaking family and never requires a formal explanation of these concepts.

As before, scheduled small and large group lessons are still given. Children may attend if they so desire. The children may also ask the teacher for a lesson at other times during the day. They may work with other children or by themselves, but all French work must be done in this specially designated area.

B. New Units to Explore

The foremost idea to keep in mind is that children enjoy what is relevant to their experience. Future vocabulary units might include things that the child likes to do outside (ex. running, playing, swimming), hobbies and work at home, the school day and its events, or activities the child does in the morning before school. Vocabulary like this is ideal for pantomime games and active dramatization.

As the children begin to read their own language, they will naturally become curious about the written form of French. The teacher may respond to their interest by writing words they know in French, or even making labels for some of the cards used on an oral level. It is important not to rush the children into reading French before they are secure in reading English.[11]

---

[11]A complete description of Montessori's language program may be found in *The Discovery of the Child* (N.Y., 1967), pp. 185-262.

PART III. APPENDICES

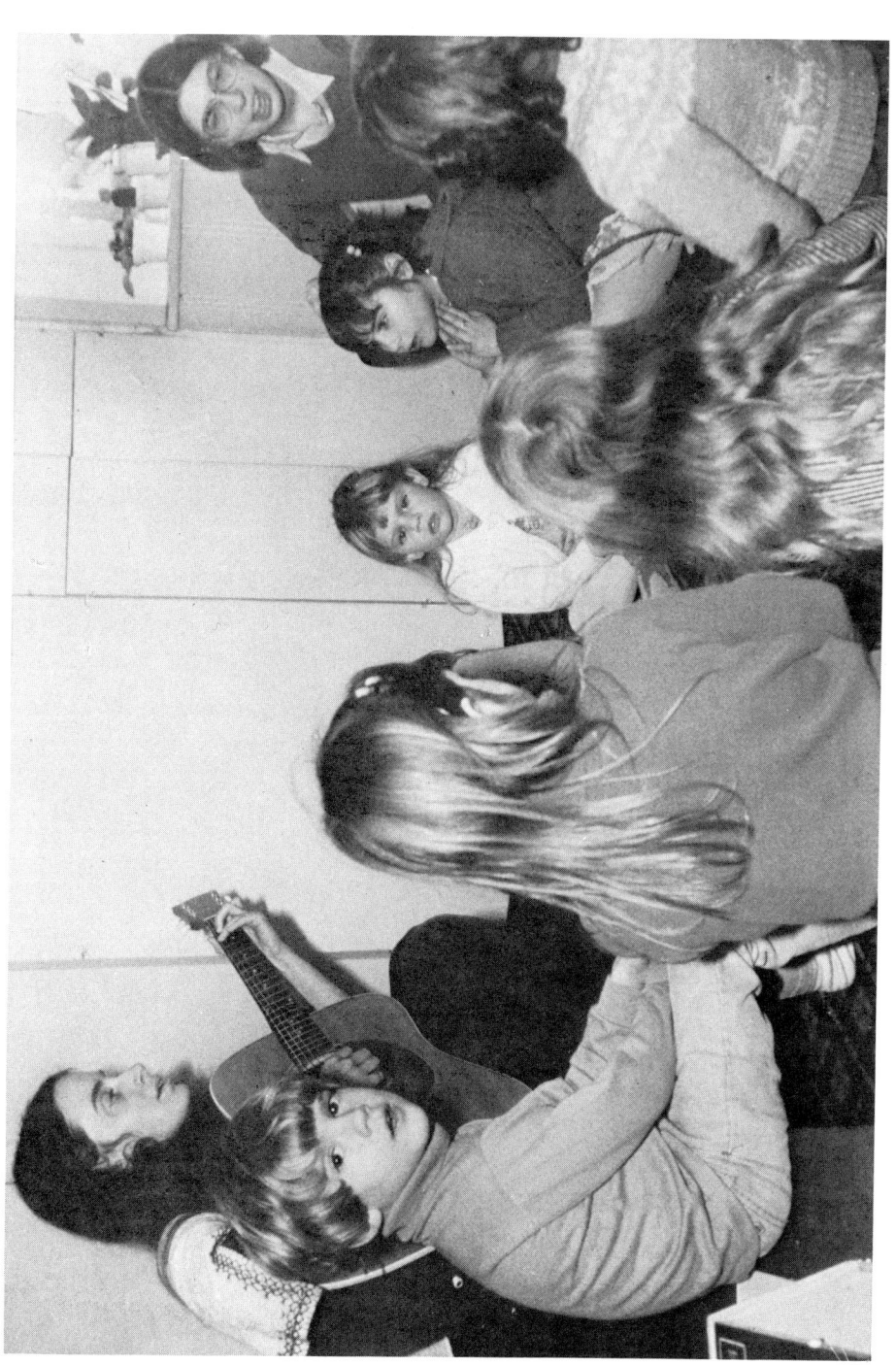

APPENDIX A

CULTURAL ACTIVITIES

1) Mardi Gras Celebration[12]

During one large group meeting (near Mardi Gras time), the history of this celebration is explained to the children. The teacher discusses the festivities of the carnival, the colorful costumes worn, and the definition of the words "Mardi Gras." ("Fat Tuesday": "Tuesday" because the holiday begins on the Tuesday before Lent; "Fat" because of the fat ox which was paraded down the Parisian streets at this time.

The children make their own masks in preparation for the party. The room is brightly decorated with streamers. During the celebration children may wear their masks and a costume if they so desire. Later, a large cake is brought out with a big foil crown on top of it. In one piece, according to Mardi Gras custom, a bean (la fève) is hidden. The child that finds the bean in his or her piece becomes king or queen of the Mardi Gras and is permitted to wear the crown. French records may be played throughout the celebration. During our carnival, we sang the well-known tune "Sur le Pont d'Avignon" and added a circle dance to the melody (see song section).

2) Trip to a bakery to watch the making of French Bread

This can easily be arranged with a local bakery. The words "le pain" may be introduced, and the process of making the bread explained by the baker. This was an extremely successful activity.

3) Trip to a French Restaurant

Although there were no French restaurants in our area within a reasonable price range, this is a trip well worth looking into. The teacher prepares by talking about various types of French food (and perhaps bringing in some samples), and by reviewing the French names of the dishes that the children have already prepared. If the trip is taken after the tea party, the children may even be able to do some of the ordering in French!

---

[12]See Ann Cole, Carolyn Haas, Elizabeth Heller, Betty Weinberger, *Children are Children are Children*, p. 39.

4) French Family Dinner

A good alternative to number 3, and a very exciting possibility, is to hold a French family dinner at the school, where the children help prepare part of the menu. Parents are invited and encouraged to bring a French "dish-to-pass."

5) Obtaining of French Pen Pals

If the children are old enough to write, they may each be given the name of a French pen pal. If they are preschoolers, the teacher may help the children compose a class letter to a single pen pal. The children may dictate questions that they would like to ask the French child and describe the activities they enjoy at home and in school. The teacher may later read and then translate the French child's response. This exercise can make the idea of another country become much more real to the children. Pen pals may be obtained by writing to any of the organizations listed in Appendix E.

6) Following a French Calendar

The French customs involved in celebrating other holidays (ex. New Year's Day, April Fool's Day, Christmas, Easter, Bastille Day) may be discussed and recreated at the proper times. The dates of these holidays may be marked on a special calendar which is posted where the children may go and look at it. The class may also follow the seasons (and the weather) and talk about what French children do on a snowy, rainy, or sunny day. Children may listen to stories about what French children like to do (see book section) and act out some of these activities.

APPENDIX B

COOKING PROJECTS

French Bread

French bread-making was an independent activity in our classroom. The materials needed for the set-up, were as follows:

- one 4' x 2' piece of vinyl or plastic—which serves as the table cover
- one mixing bowl (a wooden salad bowl is very attractive for this)
- one liquid measuring cup—taped all around at the 2/3 cup level—used to measure water
- two teaspoon measures, used to measure salt and yeast
- one wooden spoon for mixing and stirring
- two small containers with see-through covers, to hold yeast and salt (small margarine tubs are good for this)
- one scoop for flour, 1/2 cup size
- one baking pan, used for kneading the dough and for baking, approximately 8" x 10"
- for cleanups—a sponge and a dishcloth
- one container for flour (an oatmeal box is good for this)

Using a *non* water soluble marker, outline the utensils to be used.
The children wore a red/white checked baker's apron and hat while they worked.

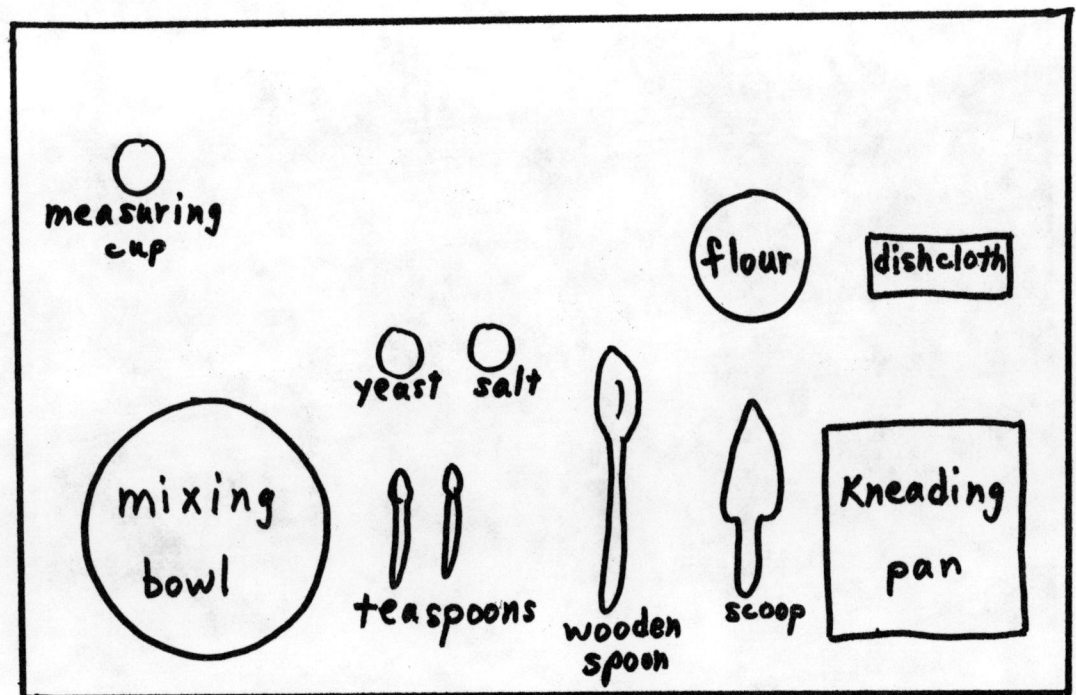

The bread recipe is as follows:

    2/3 cup lukewarm water
    1 tsp. yeast
    1 tsp "salt"   (1 part sugar to 2 parts salt. This is done to simplify the mixing process for the children and to avoid confusion arising from salt and sugar looking alike)
    1 1/2 cup flour

The procedure is as follows:

Measure 2/3 cup water into the mixing bowl. Add 1 tsp. yeast, and 1 tsp. salt into bowl. Stir until dissolved with wooden spoon. Add 3 level scoops flour, stirring after each addition, adding more if needed, to make a non-sticky dough. Form dough into a ball. Sprinkle flour onto baking pan and knead dough on pan until smooth and elastic (about 5 minutes). At this point, the dough can go into the mixing bowl to rise, or if no oven is available, into a plastic bag and into a refrigerator to be baked later. In any event, allow the dough to rise until doubled (1-2 hours) or until a finger's imprint remains in the dough, when the dough is poked. Punch down and shape into an oblong loaf. Make an 1/8" slash lengthwise across the top, with a sharp knife. Let rise until almost doubled (about 45 minutes). Brush crust with a beaten egg white mixed with water. Bake in a 400° oven 15 minutes, turn down heat to 350° and bake until crisp and browned (about 15-20 minutes longer).

The dough can remain 2-3 days in the refrigerator before baking. It may acquire a slightly sourdough-like taste (which many people like anyway).

Sweet Butter

Pour heavy sweet cream into a container with a secure lid. (A see-through container is best, in order to observe the transformation of cream to butter.) Have the children take turns shaking the cream, until it turns to butter. Serve on French Bread or crackers.

Spinach Quiche

  1 pie shell
  1 pkg. frozen spinach, defrosted (or fresh or canned if you like)
  1/2 cup swiss cheese (or other, perhaps gruyère)
  1 1/2 cups scalded milk
  3 eggs, beaten
  salt, pepper to taste

Squeeze out excess moisture from spinach (or chop and steam fresh spinach and squeeze out). Spread over bottom of pie crust. Top with grated cheese. Mix beaten eggs, scalded milk and salt and pepper to taste. Pour into shell. Bake at 350° until top is browned and custard set (about 45 minutes).
(Sauteed mushrooms or onions could be substituted for the spinach.)

Crème à la Banana

  1 medium sized banana per person
  1/2 lemon per banana (or 1 tbls. lemon juice)
  2/3 cup milk per banana
  sugar to taste

Beat the banana, lemon juice and half of the milk in a bowl until smooth. Add the rest of the milk and mix well. (For a thicker mixture, add less milk, a creamier mixture add more milk.) Add sugar (and more lemon if desired) to taste.

Truffles

    3 oz. grated unsweetened chocolate
    1/4 cup butter
    1 tsp. vanilla
    2 tbs. milk or cream
    7 tbs. confectioners sugar
    3 tbs. ground nuts

Melt the grated chocolate and butter together. Remove from heat. Stir in vanilla and milk. Add sugar and nuts and stir until smooth. Refrigerate a few hours (or until next day). Roll small teaspoonfull in palm of hand to form balls. Roll these in chocolate shots, or powdered sugar, or coconut, etc.

It is especially exciting for children to see how their lives have been influenced already by French culture. Commonplace French foods, such as omelettes, crêpes, petits-fours can be identified as being French, and prepared with the children.

APPENDIX C

SONGS

Bonjour Mes Amis
(to the tune of "Shalom Chaverim")

2. Au revoir mes amis, au revoir mes amis
   Au revoir, au revoir
   Au revoir mes amis, au revoir mes amis
   Au revoir, au revoir

To teach "Levez-vous" and "Asseyez-vous" the following verses may be used:

Levez-vous mes amis, Asseyez-vous mes amis
   Levez-vous, Asseyez-vous
Levez-vous mes amis, asseyez-vous mes amis
   Levez-vous, Asseyez-vous.

The children may follow the commands given in the song.

Sur le Pont d'Avignon

PRESENTATION:

(We made up a little dance to go with the song, and used a guitar accompaniment.)

1. A translation of the words is given to the children. The teacher explains that the bridge is found in France, but that it is a very old bridge and that now only half of it is standing.

    Translation: On the bridge of Avignon
    Everybody dances, everybody dances
    On the bridge of Avignon
    Everybody dances in a circle.

2. The dance may be done as follows: Two children hold up their arms to form a bridge. The other children hold hands to form a circle; part of this circle will pass under the arms of the two "bridge" children. The children in the circle proceed to skip around and to in turn go under the bridge while they are singing the song.

Alouette

Here is a well-known French song that we adapted to fit the body parts we learned:

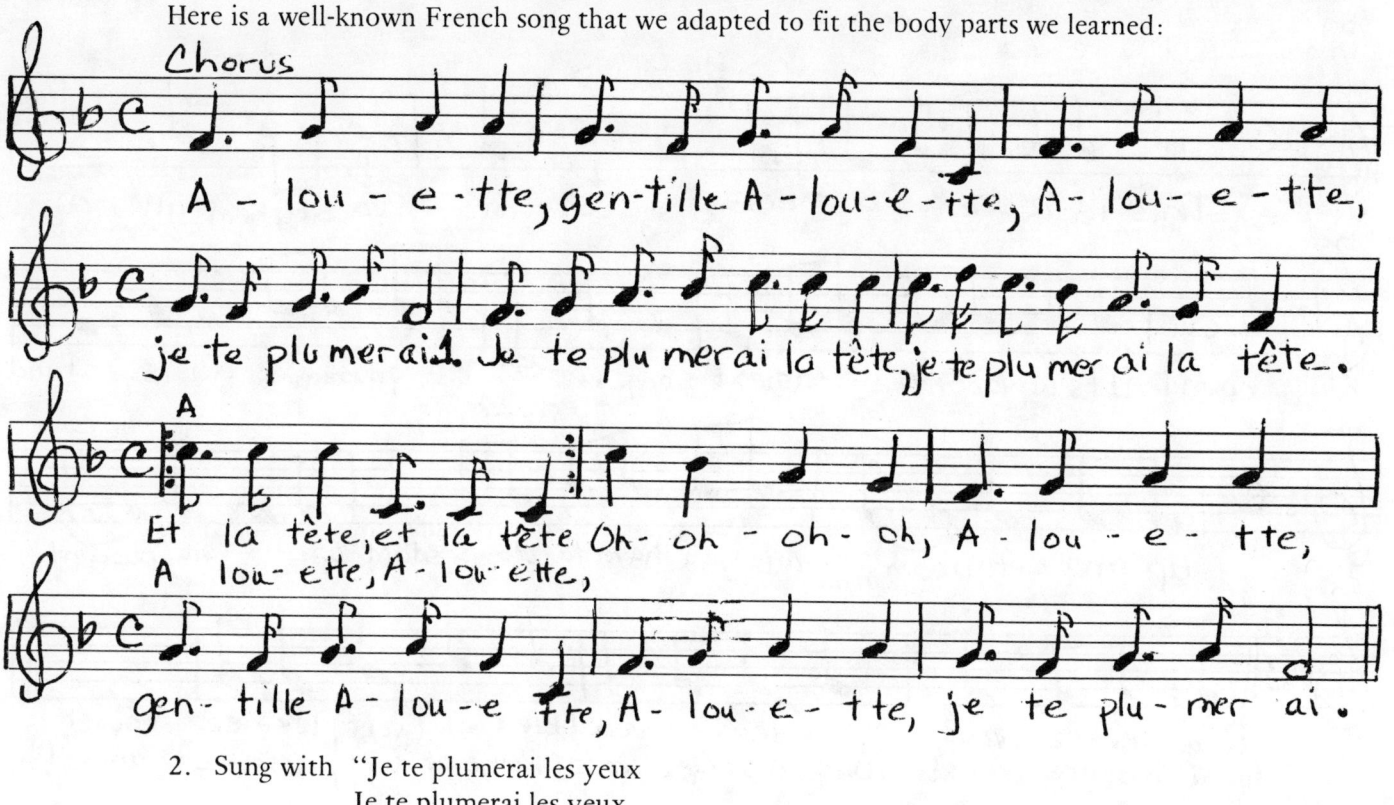

2. Sung with "Je te plumerai les yeux
   Je te plumerai les yeux
   Et la tête
   Et la tête
   Alouette
   Alouette
   Oh-oh-oh-oh, etc."

   Part A is repeated as needed

3. Verses may be sung with "Je te plumerai le nez, la bouche, et le cou," reversing the order when the singers arrive at part A.

PRESENTATION:

1. The teacher goes over the translation with the children, phrase by phrase.
   "Alouette"--meadowlark (a kind of bird)
   "Gentille Alouette"--nice meadowlark
   "Je te plumerai"--I will defeather you
2. One of the children made up the following motions to the song. When the word "alouette" is sung, the children flap their elbows like the wings of a bird. When "Je te plumerai" is sung, the children pretend to pluck out the feathers. When a part of the body is mentioned, the children point to that part of the body.

Colors Song[13]

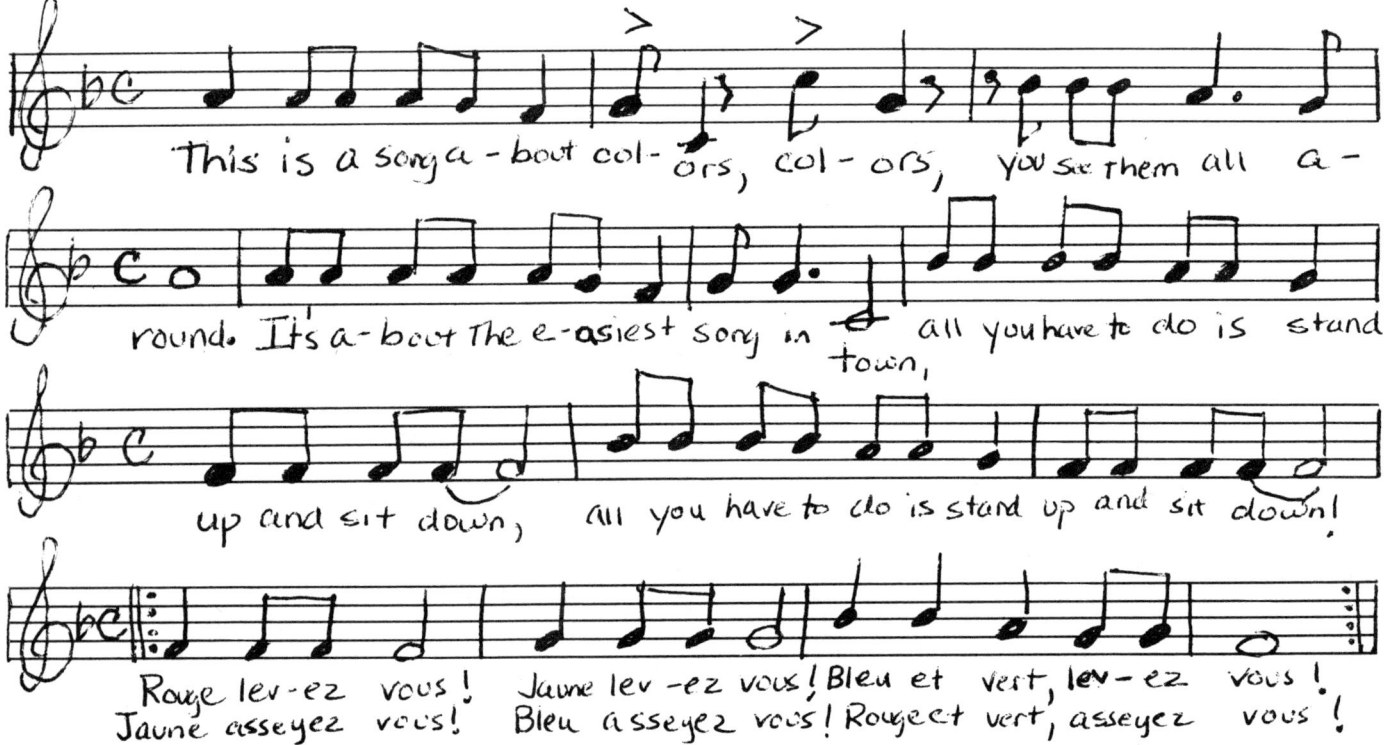

CHORUS

2. Rouge, levez-vous
   Bleu, levez-vous
   Orange et Vert, levez-vous

   Orange, asseyez-vous
   Bleu-asseyez-vous
   Jaune et Bleu, levez-vous

[13]Adapted from the Hap Palmer song "Colors" (*Learning Basic Skills Through Music*, vol. 1, Educational Activities, Inc., Freeport, N.Y. 11520)

CHORUS

(Other verses may be invented)

PRESENTATION:

1. The teacher reviews the color vocabulary and the commands "Levez-vous" and "Asseyez-vous" with the children.

2. The children hold the balloons they were given after reading the story "The Red Balloon." When they hear their color in the song, they must follow the command given.

APPENDIX D

BOOKS FOR CHILDREN

de Brunhoff, Laurent. *Babar's French Lessons (Les Leçons de Français de Babar)*. New York: Random House, 1963.

    Portions of this book may supplant the vocabulary lessons. While the text needs some editing for preschool children, this book, with its bright illustrations, was enjoyed by all.

Douglas, Marjory Stoneman. *The Key to Paris*. New York: J. B. Lippincott Company, 1961.

    This book contains appealing black and white photos and describes part of Paris and various Parisian specialties. The text, while more appropriate for older children, could be paraphrased and simplified by the teacher.

Harris, Leon A. *Young France (Children of France at Work and Play)*. New York: Dodd, Mead and Co., 1964.

    This book describes French schools, sports, families, holidays, and so on. The text deals with material of interest to young children, but may need to be paraphrased and slightly shortened for the preschool child.

Joslin, Sesyle and John Alcorn. *La Petite Famille*. New York: Harcourt, Brace and World, Inc., 1964.

    The text of this book is written in French and gives vocabulary from both family and food units. Although the children will probably not have learned many of the words in the text, sections of this book are definitely worth using as a teaching aid. The illustrations are amusing and brightly colored.

Lamorisse, Albert. *The Red Balloon*. New York: Doubleday & Co., Inc., 1956.

    An excellent story which will hold the child's interest again and again.

Sasek, Miroslav. *This is Paris*. New York: The Macmillan Co., 1959.

    Here a Czech artist paints his impressions of Paris. This work is excellent for young children, as the author presents Paris as a child might see it. It is a nice blend of information done in storybook style, with pictures of markets, cats, lampposts, painters, and boats; all colorfully presented.

von Hippel, Ursula. *Toute Ma Famille*. New York: Coward-McCann, Inc.

    An excellent choice for review of family vocabulary. This work has a very simple text, quite suitable for our program.

Wallace, John A. *Getting to Know France*. New York: Coward-McCann, Inc., 1962.

    This work has an appealing text for older children (ages 9-11) but may be edited for the preschool child. The illustrations are well-done and the choice of topics well-balanced.

Weiss, Hugh. *A Week in Daniel's World: France*. New York: Crowell-Collier Press, 1969.

    An excellent description of a French boy's family life, interests, and activities. The children really enjoyed this one.

APPENDIX E

PEN PAL ORGANIZATIONS*

1. International Federation of Organizations for School Correspondence and Exchange
   29 Rue d'Ulm
   F-75005 Paris, France

2. International Friendship League
   40 Mount Vernon Street
   Boston, MA 02108

3. League of Friendship (for pen pals ages 12-22)
   P.O. Box 509
   Mt. Vernon, OH 43050

   (50 cents for services, send a stamped, self-addressed envelope)

4. Letters Abroad (for pen pals over 15)
   209 E. 56th Street
   New York, N.Y. 10022

   (A stamped, self-addressed envelope is requested)

5. Student Letter Exchange (for pen pals ages 10-19)
   RFD No. 4
   Waseca, MN, 56093

   (65 cents per name. All correspondence is in English)

6. World Pen Pals (for pen pals ages 12-20)
   1690 Como Avenue
   St. Paul, MN 55108

   (one dollar for individual pen pals, special group rates available)

---

*Source: *Encyclopedia of Associations: Volume 1. National Organizations of the U.S.* Gale Research Company, Book Tower, Detroit, Michigan, 48226 USA: 1979.

APPENDIX F

BOOKS FOR REFERENCE

Cole, Ann, Haas, Carolyn, Heller, Elizabeth and Weinberger, Betty. *Children are Children are Children*. U.S.A.: Little Brown & Co., 1978.

Hainstock, Elizabeth G. *The Essential Montessori*. U.S.A.: The New American Library Inc., 1978.

Hilgard, Ernest R., Atkinson, Richard C., and Atkinson, Rita L. *Introduction to Psychology*. U.S.A.: Harcourt, Brace, Jovanovich, Inc., 1975.

Montessori, Maria. *The Discovery of the Child*. New York: Ballantine Books, Inc., 1967.